AN EARLY HISTORY OF THE MARS HILL CHURCH OF CHRIST

With a Collection of Memories by Members of the Congregation

C. WAYNE KILPATRICK

Preface by
RICKEY COLLUM

Blackberry Books

Copyright © 2024 by Mars Hill Church of Christ

ISBN 978-1-956811-61-2 (pbk) ; 978-1-956811-62-9 (ebook)

All rights reserved.

No part of this book may be reproduced in any form or by any electronic or mechanical means, including information storage and retrieval systems, without written permission from the author, except for the use of brief quotations in a book review.

Typesetting and book design by Blackberry Books.

Contents

Preface v

1. A HISTORY OF MARS HILL CHURCH OF CHRIST 1
   C. Wayne Kilpatrick
2. AN ARTICLE 59
   T. B. Larimore
3. REMINISCENCES OF MARS HILL CHURCH OF CHRIST 62
   Kenneth Davis interviewing Mr. Virgil Larimore
4. History of Mars Hill Church of Christ 67
5. MY TENURE AT MARS HILL 70
   Randy Baker
6. A CHURCH THAT BEGAN BECAUSE OF HARRASEMENT 72
   Jack Wilhelm
7. Mars Hill Is Added to Alabama Register 76
8. A LETTER 78
   Nelson Sparks
9. MARS HILL CHURCH MEMORIES 80
   Julia Buffler
10. OUR HISTORY 84
    Rion Golden
11. Memories 86
12. Enrollment 96
13. List of Ministers 110
14. Photographs 112
15. Paintings of the Old Building by Various Artists 123

Preface

In July of 2023, I became the preacher of Mars Hill church of Christ, I had been a member for thirteen years and served as a deacon for seven of those years. My wife has been the church secretary for twenty-seven years. We raised both of our sons in this congregation. So, I have a history with this church.

Coming back as a preacher to this church that I love, I understand two things, 1.) I stand on the shoulders of giants. The preachers who came before me were some of the most profound of their day. I am in awe when I read the names and the accomplishments of those who served before me. I can never be the preacher they were and can only strive to live up to their examples. 2.) The second thing I know is that I love the history of the people who have worshipped at Mars Hill church of Christ. This is why we have compiled this book on the history of what is called, by the Mars Hill congregation as "the old building." When you mention "church history" my friend, Wayne

Kilpatrick will appear like a genie out of the bottle. Wayne has forgotten more about church history than most scholars will ever know. Wayne provided the largest part of this book from notes he had collected through the years.

When we first came to Mars Hill in 1994, the then preacher, Randy Baker, showed us the "old building." I have always been a fan of architecture, and that is the first thing you notice. The large tray ceiling takes your eye, followed by the podium and the pot-bellied stove. But, when you finally can speak, all that goes away because the acoustics of that building built in 1904 will create a memory you will never forget. This began my love of the "old building." I remember asking why it was called the "old building" and the answer was that the building that was built in 1969, will forever be "the new building."

From that day forward whenever I got an opportunity, I would corner one of the older members, some of whom had always been a member of Mars Hill, and extract any memory of "the old building when it was the "new building." I would talk to Cris Moore, who had served as an elder there and had been a member for over 70 years. He would tell of old men sitting at the back of the church so that they could spit tobacco juice out the transom windows. He shared that the first service he performed for the Lord was to hold the trace chains on the mules outside so that the people inside could hear the preacher. While playing Rook, I would ask my partner, Julia Buffler, a lifelong member of Mars Hill church of Christ, about what it was like back then, and she told me of her baptism in the curve of the creek that ran alongside the building. I loved talking to her and must confess that I would get so enthralled by her stories that I now cannot remember them at all.

In 1999, a short time after we came to Mars Hill, they built the annex/fellowship hall. This gave me more time to be around the people who are the history of Mars Hill. To carry on that history, it was decided that a fireplace would be the center of the fellowship hall and that the stones of that fireplace would come from the creek where Mars Hill church of Christ was established.

Rickey Collum

A History of Mars Hill Church of Christ

C. WAYNE KILPATRICK

The history of the Mars Hill church began with Stony Point. During Union occupation travelling to Stony Point and back to the Mars Hill community was many times very difficult. Chisholm Road was a main artery to Clifton, Tennessee where most of the Union military supplies were offloaded from boats and hauled down to Florence. The Chisholm Road was heavily guarded. Many times the Christians, and especially the Gresham family, from Mars Hill had to cross that road to attend worship at Stony Point. Brethren from communities east of Chisholm Road were turned back. This caused this family and their Christian neighbors, who were members at Stony Point, to start worshipping in their homes. Their numbers grew to the point that after the war they decided not to return to Stony Point but rather establish a congregation in their community.

The brethren secured the use of an abandoned church building from the Methodists. It was known as

"Hopewell." Brother J. H. Dunn preached occasionally at Hopewell, as well as at Stony Point and in the Middle Cypress community. Upon his first visit to Hopewell, he wrote:

> A New Family Gathered For The Lord. Lone Mulberry, Ala., Oct. 5, 1867. Bros. Fanning and Lipscomb: On last Saturday I commenced a meeting at Hopewell meeting house, near Florence, Ala., which continued up to Thursday. We had quite an interesting time, this being a new field, where our brethren hitherto have preached but little. I immersed six during the interview three of each sex, two of them heads of families-one from the Methodists, one from the Baptists, and one or perhaps two from the mourners' bench. They have enrolled their names and pledged themselves to watch over each other for good, and to keep the ordinances of God's house faithfully. They number twenty-six, and the prospects for additions are flattering.
>
> Hopewell is situated on the Military or Nashville Road four and a half miles north of Florence. It is a neat, well-finished frame house, of good size. It is a neat well-finished house of good size. It was built by and belonged to the Methodists, and for some cause, they offered it for sale, and two of our liberal brethren and a good sister became the purchasers, paid for it, and have a deed to it.
>
> Preachers are affectionately solicited of man-to call and preach for them. Inquire for Bro. John A. Thompson or Bro. Andrew J. Gresham, who reside near the meeting house either of whom will gladly

receive a preacher and entertain him and will not send him away empty. Your old and devoted brother in the one hope, J. H. Dunn. *Gospel Advocate* (October 24, 1867): 859.

By May 31, 1868, the brethren had bought the building from the Methodists. *Deed Book—1867* (Lauderdale County Courthouse, Florence, Alabama): 580–581.

It was to this congregation that T.B. Larimore came to hold a meeting in June of 1868. Srygley described Hopewell as being four miles from Florence, and scarcely more than a stone's throw from Mars Hill. (*Larimore And His Boys*, 1889: 98). The brethren did not think Larimore preached well enough, so they took him cross the county to Brother Young's (Thomas W. Young) house to preach. Larimore wrote of this event at Hopewell:

> I came to Hopewell to hold a protracted meeting (June 1868). They let me try to preach once, and they were so pleased with that 'sarmint' that they let me off—suddenly! The meeting closed with a jerk and a bang. It was not wound up much, hence required but little time to run down; or perhaps it ran down so very fast is why it struck bottom so quick. It was wound up for eight days and it ran down in an hour. An Irishman once said: "They thuck me into the charch for six months on trial; but I did so well they let me off in three months.' Hopewell did better by me than that—they took me for eight days and let me off in sixty minutes. Well, they did exactly right. They reasoned

thus: 'We have had none but good preachers here; we are few and weak; our enemies hold the fort and camp on the field. Now, if we let *him* try to preach here, it is goodbye to our prospects. Better have no preaching than his sort.' Then they said: "What shall we do with him? This will we do—Brother and sister Young live a way back—good preachers rarely go there; they will appreciate any kind of preaching; to them will we send him.' They said to me: 'We will take you to Bro. Young's; he and sister Young and Frank and another one or two are the church there; they are good people and will treat you well.' They sent me—I believe Bro. Andrew Gresham took in a buggy. *Larimore And His Boys*, (1889): 34.

Brother Andrew Gresham (one of Larimore's future brothers-in-law) drove Larimore in a buggy to Thomas Young's house. The result of Larimore's trip to the Youngs was the establishment of the Middle Cypress congregation, from what had been, up until this time, a house church. Middle Cypress will be discussed with the Bethelberry congregation.

Larimore, perhaps unknowingly, pointed out a weakness at Hopewell. He wrote:

This congregation is small but devoted to their Master's cause. They never learned to wait for the preacher to come around to serve the Lord for them; but, like valiant soldiers of the cross, they are ever at their post. They meet every first day of the week, preacher, or no preacher, and spend usually, three hours or more in teaching the children, reading the

Holy Scriptures, exhorting each other in psalms, hymns, and spiritual songs, in breaking of bread, and in prayers. *Gospel Advocate*, (August 19, 1869): 784—785.

The weakness was their numerical strength. They never seemed to grow in number. The congregation had already begun to make plans to relocate to another site. The brethren continued to meet at the Hopewell site until 1871 when they relocated to the old foundry building near Mars Hill College [the site of the present-day congregation].

Larimore and the brethren had heard that someone intended to buy the old foundry property and start a brewery. So, Larimore and the brethren approached the owner of the property and purchased it. They began remodeling the old foundry building and fashioned it into a reasonably good meeting house. It was at this time the congregation took on the name "Mars Hill church of Christ." They occupied the newly renovated building sometime late in 1870. Srygley gives the date—1870 as when the brethren began using the foundry building (F.B. Srygley, *Letters and Sermons*, vol II, Nashville: McQuiddy Printing Company, 44).

Brother Granville Lipscomb mentioned a meeting that he held at Hopewell on the 2nd and 3rd Lord's days in August 1871, which contradicts Srygley's statement.

Apparently Srygley got several dates wrong in his book *Larimore and His Boys*. Lipscomb wrote:

> Brother David. We had the pleasure of attending a series of meetings held by the brothers and sisters

meeting at Hopewell five miles North East of Florence Ala., commencing the 2nd. and 3rd. Lord's days in August. The meeting closed with 18 accessions, 10 by baptism, 4 from the Baptists, 3 by commendation, and one from the Presbyterians, yet unbaptized. The cause seems to be advancing rapidly in this section. The brethren and sisters meet every Lord's day to attend the ordinances; they have much to encourage them; we trust they will continue zealous in the good cause ...G. Lipscomb. *Gospel Advocate* (August 31, 1871): 798-99.

In 1874 Larimore married John Eaton Campbell to Miss Annie Wade. The ceremony took place at Mars Hill. This was reported in Annie's obituary and it is the only thing recorded at Mars Hill for that entire year. *Gospel Advocate* (October 22, 1914): 1114.

For us to write as complete a history of this congregation as we can, we must consider Mars Hill College's history. The history of the congregation is closely tied to the history of Mars Hill College. Therefore, to retrieve the congregation's history, we must also look at the school's history.

We began this connection with a report on an event that shows the concern members at Mars Hill had for their fellowman. Larimore represented the congregation well. The following account confirms this:

Prof. Larimore. This gentleman, by his course during the late epidemic acquired a high position in the hearts of the people of Florence. When our people did not know where to turn for safety, and when many kind-hearted country people would not permit a person from Florence to alight at their doors, Mr. Larimore welcomed all who came to him and furnished them houses at Mars Hill, free of charge. Of the ninety persons who sojourned at Mars Hill during the fever in Florence, not one was sick or died. This speaks volumes for the health of Mars Hill. We wish Mr. Larimore every success in his school. The Christian church should sustain it fully. Florence, Ala., Gazette. *Gospel Advocate* (January 2, 1879): 11.

The second report to appear in the *Gospel Advocate*, after the congregation relocated from the Hopewell site to Mars Hill was sent by F. D. Srygley, a student at the school, but also a member of the Mars Hill church of Christ:

Bro. Larimore reached home Saturday night about midnight. He has added about 130 to the church since July 15. I met him at church Lord's day morning; the first time I had seen him since July 1. After a warm greeting, he opened his Bible, and, pointing to a passage in the sixth chapter of John, said, "Did you ever notice this," He then gave me a new and brilliant idea, after which he continued in a voice that trembled with emotion, "Oh, this blessed book? I wish I could tear my mind from every other subject and make it my constant and only study for life." I relate this to show his manner of teaching the Bible. Whether in school or out he modestly communicated every idea he thinks a student will appreciate and utilize. Brethren, this Institution, especially the Bible

College, is doing much for the church. We have many good schools—probably more than we can support. If any must perish let us have those that do most for Christianity. If the preservation of our best schools will not save Mars Hill, I shall try to be reconciled to the death of my Alma Mater ... *Gospel Advocate* (October 9, 1879): 646.

This report gave two interesting facts. 1. Larimore's style of teaching and preaching. 2. Confirms Larimore's working with the Mars Hill congregation while at home. Larimore seemingly refers to the work at the Mars Hill church:

T. B Larimore writes from Mars Hill College near Florence, Ala., Oct. 13, 1879: Our Mars' Hill work has begun. Two confessions, yesterday Bro. Clayton (J. C.) McQuiddy has just returned from Mountain Mill-three accessions, one over three score and ten. *Gospel Advocate* (October 23, 1879): 683.

When school began each session, Larimore was working, mostly, for the school and the Mars Hill congregation. So, "Our Mars Hill work has begun" is to be understood as both school and church at Mars Hill.

In late Spring of 1880 Robert Wallace (R.W.) Officer was raising money for his mission work amongst the Indians. He traveled throughout North Alabama and South Middle Tennessee preparing for his mission work amongst the Indians. In the Fall of 1880, he moved to Texas where he began full-time work with the Gainesville Church of Christ. This was the beginning of his work among the Indians north of the Red River in Indian Territory (Oklahoma) where he distributed books, papers, and tracts with the aid of an interpreter. Officer came to the Florence area and to Mars Hill in June and preached a few sermons. He also brought T. C. Biles, a disenchanted Methodist preacher, with him. While at Mars Hill Officer baptized Biles and gave the following report:

> Bro. Biles made the good confession, and I baptized him at Mars' Hill. He went to Florence and began preaching in the City Hall. His congregation grew through the week at night. I spent the rest of my time with Bro. M. Askew, preaching at night at his house: Returned to Mars' Hill, Lord's day and preached for the brethren in the morning; one young man came forward and made the good confession, and went with me to Bro. Askew's 10 miles below on Tennessee River where I preached at 7 o'clock Lord's day evening, where 7 others confessed the Lord Jesus. All were buried with the Lord, filled the grave that Jesus left empty, and arose by faith in the promise. We found Bro. T. B. Larimore, all the faculty, and all the young men working together for good. One of the essentials there, is the untiring labors of sister Larimore ... Yours in hope, R.W. O. Lewisburg, Tenn., June 7, 1880. *Gospel Advocate* (July 1, 1880): 423.

Officer was a diligent missionary and won the hearts of many people in Alabama and Tennessee. He was especially loved by the Mars Hill congregation.

Our next insight into the work at Mars Hill came

from H. H. Turner, one of "Larimore's boys." The report read thus:

> Probably a few items from this part of the Lord's vineyard will be interesting to the many readers of the Advocate, especially to the Mars Hill people as I am from there myself. I am the evangelist through this section of country, sent out by the Mars Hill congregation. I have been at work now six months, during which time I have not failed to declare the counsel of God. Though, occasionally I have been shut out of the church and school houses of the sects, on such occasions I preach in the grove, or some man's house. I was told by one old lady not long ago that I was worse than the devil, for when was resisted, he would flee; but the more I was resisted the more I would contend and preach. Since Christmas I have preached one hundred and ten discourses, or times. Preached at twenty different points, or places. I have disposed of about a. thousand tracts and Hymnbooks. I have had thirty-five additions. And the field is white, ready to harvest, hundreds are perishing for the bread of life. We need more evangelists in this part of the Lord's vineyard. There are congregations and brethren enough in this section, to have out three or four regular evangelists all the time, if they would. Out of eight or ten congregations, there is only one that is doing anything of that kind; that is my home or Mars Hill congregation, the bright and shining light; most the least congregation but doing more than all the rest. Now there are wealthy brethren in some of these congregations that are able to do much towards

sustaining an evangelist. Will some of the brethren take hold of it and get them to work together? For my part, I am busy working in destitute places. Brethren, do not sleep always, arise from your lethargy; go to work, work for Jesus, then He will own and bless your labors.—H. H. Turner, Florence, Ala., July 4, 1883. *Gospel Advocate* (July 18, 1883): 458.

One of the editors at the *Gospel Advocate* wrote the following:

"I had good news to tell, and was determined to tell it," Bro. Turner says, was the inspiration to him to labor under difficulties. Earnestness is worth a thousand-fold more in reaching men with the gospel, than eloquence or learning. The Mars Hill church last year, helping Bro. Turner, added one hundred and nine persons to the Lord, planted five young congregations, kept three Sunday-schools at work in a destitute and needy field. Mars Hill is a weak congregation, financially and numerically. Who can show a better record? Mars Hill congregation could not have brought a preacher from a distance and sustained him, but an earnest man living close by, with the help he could get in the field of labor, was supported. The way to clean the street is for everyone to sweep before his own door. The way to convert the world, ill for every church and every Christian to convert his neighbors. The Mars Hill church is a good example to other churches in Alabama and everywhere. *Gospel Advocate* (February 20, 1884): 119.

That same year Turner gave another report on this mission-minded congregation. He reported on the work sponsored by Mars Hill. Under the heading of "A Commendable Example," he wrote:

> The church at Mars Hill Ala., collects through its regular contributions, such sum as it can, and sends a couple of young preachers to the nearest destitute section to labor so long as they can on the support given. In July or August, it started two out a foot. The last report gives sixty-seven baptisms as the result. Why will not other churches do likewise? Scarcely a church in the land but can do as much if it will. *Gospel Advocate* (September 17, 1884): 603.

These three articles demonstrate the concern for lost souls and the determination to do something about it at Mars Hill. It would be two more years before another report came forth in the *Gospel Advocate*. T. B. Larimore writes:

> My homework for the present closes with the writing of Bro. Wade's obituary: He was a devoted personal friend of mine. One of the best friends of the needy I have ever known. He read the Bible and the Advocate, seemed to care for no other paper, no other book. I enter the evangelistic field tomorrow, to evangelize ill Jan. 1, 1887, 'the Lord willing.' Our month's work at Mars Hill and Florence resulted in great good. *Gospel Advocate* (May 26, 1886): 331.

The Wade mentioned by Larimore was John D.

Wade of the Antioch congregation near present-day Iron City, Tennessee. Wade had a terrible accident and one of his arms was torn off at his gristmill on Wolf Creek and died a few days later. *Gospel Advocate* (May 26, 1886): 331. He was one of the strongest supporters of Mars Hill College and a very close friend to Larimore. Larimore's report concerning his work at the Mars Hill church was supported in another segment of the *Gospel Advocate* by Brown Godwin:

> Bro. Larimore closed his school with a series of meetings at Mars Hill and at Florence. Last report said 10 accessions. Meeting still going on. Bro. Larimore aims to teach 10- or 12-weeks next year. Brethren remember this school is striving to teach pure religion, will you help, or will you send your children to sectarian schools or to others that only try to get them through their books. This school will begin in January; therefore, you can go to school and then cultivate a crop. Those preparing for preaching will find this to be the place for them.—Brown Godwin, Linden, Tenn. *Gospel Advocate* (May 26, 1886): 331.

For some unknown reason, nothing was printed in the *Gospel Advocate*, relating to the work of the church at Mars Hill, for five years. A report about Larimore's work as an evangelist finally broke the silence. The *Gospel Advocate* printed part of a letter that Larimore had written:

> Bro. Larimore is now at home, Mars' Hill, near Florence, Ala. In a private letter he says, "I am

preaching for the home folks every night and Sunday too. There is no rest for the weary—in this world." He will begin a meeting with Campbell Street church, Louisville, Ky., the first Sunday in April—possibly a few days earlier. *Gospel Advocate* (March 25, 1891): 186.

Later, in October the *Gospel Advocate* printed an excerpt from another private letter of Larimore's and it gave another bit of information on the Mars Hill church work. It was a letter from Eddie Blalock in which Larimore pointed out facts about the Blalock families' involvement with the church at Mars Hill. We take the liberty to give a few facts from this letter:

> Bro. Larimore encloses for me a letter from Eddie Blaylock, whom I (F. B. Srygley) knew as a little boy studying "second reader" and trying to learn the "multiplication table" a few years ago at Mars' Hill. On the margin of this letter in Bro. Larimore's well-known writing I find these words: 'Eddie is not only one of the Mars' Hill boys, but one of our neighbor boys. His father is a deacon in our home congregation, and one of the best of men. I prophesy good concerning Eddie.' I understand that "Eddie" graduated from the Florence State Normal College after Mars' Hill College was suspended. He was one of the small boys then. He is now teaching at Mountain Mills and making himself useful in the vineyard of the Lord as well. May the Lord bless him. *Gospel Advocate* (October 14. 1891): 649–650.

This lets us peek into the private lives of a family

very much involved in the work at Mars Hill (and members of that family still are involved with the Mars Hill work, presently [2024]).

In December of that year, Larimore reported on another member at the Mars Hill congregation. This time it was an elder at Mars Hill that he gave a report. It was Larimore's brother-in-law W. H. Gresham. Larimore wrote:

> Bro. W. H. Gresham, whom all our Mars Hill boys and girls remember, of course, as one of our faithful Mars Hill elders, has just closed a three days' meeting at Stony Point, resulting in fourteen accessions to that patient congregation that, in the bitter-sweet long-ago, suffered so many of 'the boys' to 'make a beginning' there. Patient, long-suffering, 'Old Stony' is still solid. *Gospel Advocate* (December 10, 1891): 780.

This report shows the close ties between Mars Hill and Stony Point. Remember that Mars Hill was formed out of Stony Point during the Civil War. Families in both congregations were related. This bond still exists in 2024.

The next report we give in full. It contains so much information about the church and community it deserves full attention:

> Private Letter from Bro. Larimore. [The following letter was not intended for publication, but we take the liberty of publishing it, thinking it will be of interest to many of our readers. Ed.]
>
> Our all-day meeting at Mars' Hill yesterday was

delightfully pleasant. A joyous reunion of families and friends. Two discourses and one dinner, of course. The L. & N. R. R. contributed much to the success of the meeting by furnishing comfortable conveyance to and from Mars' Hill. Iron City, West Point and St. Joe sent a special train to Mars' Hill, "literally packed with people—men, women and children— from engine to rear platform." The youngest visitor from afar was "the charming little Miss" Anonymous Myers, of Iron City, whose age, according to the "official report" and record thereof, was (is) six weeks and seven days. The oldest was — old. "The tariff question, of which you have heard or seen some mention in political papers or elsewhere, has been so learnedly, logically, lengthily, thoroughly and frequently expounded and discussed in these favored parts of our great country recently, that I think the railroad authorities wisely and generously allowed the seven-week-old customer to be "put on the free list." This is not "official," however—simply my opinion. For various reasons, one of the most seriously important of which was that I had just been compelled to close a meeting at Mooresville when the interest demanded its continuance, I was in no condition to perform my part of the programme; but I did the best I could, and the people possessed too much magnanimity of soul to tell me what they thought. This is one of the many marvelous blessings vouchsafed to preachers here below. Few things can crush me more completely than to be compelled to close a meeting when the most joyous and glorious results are at hand, and few have been more frequently thus crushed than I. I have long been promising myself, among other things, these three: 1. To rest a few weeks, in the warmest part of every year. Faithful friends who love me earnestly entreat me to do so, and I believe duty to myself demands it; but how can I? All this year, I have been preaching twice or thrice a day, and, yet how little I have done! How much needs to be done, and that without delay! "Some sweet day," we shall "pass over the river and rest under the shade of the trees." "Meet me there." 2. To never make or agree to any engagement or arrangement that promises to compel me to close a meeting before it ought to be closed—to have but one engagement at a time and fight every fight to a finish; but it is so hard for me to say no! In all these years of tearful toil, I have never finished but one meeting. I work at one place as long as other engagements and positive promises will permit and then go elsewhere, instead of remaining at each place as long as the interest demands. The latter is evidently the correct way. The former is the way I do. 3. To build at Mars' Hill, just such a church house as ought to be here, for all time, viz: A commodious, solid-stone structure; not fine, fashionable and showy, but neat, plain, substantial, comfortable and durable. A house that will stand for ages and always be appreciated by the humble workers and worshipers "in the vineyard of the Lord." Few know how we have struggled, how we have economized, or what we need here; yet the name and place are near and dear—almost sacred—to thousands who love the Lord, his people and his cause. When the railroad that has done so much to elevate and almost make this country was completed and Mars' Hill was made a station— not a post-office, however, Florence still being our post-office—the authorities, as a compliment to me, changed the name from Mars' Hill to Larimore; but, though I appreciated their kindness and the compliment, I immediately appealed to them to reverse their decision and rescue from "oblivion" the name by which the place has so long been known; and, though Larimore, instead of Mars' Hill was on their time tables, etc., they graciously and generously granted my request, and thus has been preserved, perhaps perpetuated the name Mars' Hill.—T. B. Larimore. Mars' Hill, Ala., Sept. 5,' 92. *Gospel Advocate* (September 15, 1892): 583.

Larimore's refusal to accept the new name "Larimore" for the train station near Mars Hill, shows his modesty and no desire to be honored in that way. But the battle shifted to brethren thinking Mars Hill had a post office. That was not Larimore's desire either. He wrote a short request to the brethren and pleaded with them that there was not a post office at Mars Hill. It read as follows:

Will you please tell them again that Mars Hill is not, never has been, and probably never is to be, a post office? Some letters addressed to me at Mars' Hill reach me, after long delay—how, I do not know. Ten times as many may never reach me. Of course, the writers feel about them just as if they knew I received them on time. Mars' Hill is simply a suburb of Florence, and Florence is our post office—Box E — T. B. Larimore. *Gospel Advocate* (October 13, 1892): 648.

Larimore was in such high demand to hold meetings he had to mark off August for the annual meeting at his own home, Mars' Hill. The following report reveals this:

> He is now at Winchester, Tenn., and he has set apart August for the annual meeting at his own home, Mars' Hill, near Florence, Ala. The Mars Hill meeting is attended every year by more or less visitors from different parts of the country, and those who propose to attend this year may make their arrangements to go sometime in August. While at home he will probably do some preaching at other points in that part of Alabama, as he does every year, and then, by the blessing of God he will begin another series of evangelistic labors in the early fall, which will probably continue without cessation from point to point till the end of the year .... He should always be addressed at Florence, Ala. His mail is forwarded regularly from Florence, no matter where he may be. *Gospel Advocate* (July 6, 1893), 430.

His popularity as an evangelist is one reason for his closing of Mars Hill College. Another was that he was getting burned out from constantly having to raise funds for the school. He believed he could be more effective as an evangelist than he could as a schoolteacher. This writer believes he made a bad mistake. Looking at the results of his school shows that he multiplied himself hundreds of times and the proof is the churches that were established by his "boys." Basil Overton had a saying: "I love what I'm doing because I don't know what I'm doing"—meaning we never know the results of the work we do. "Blessed are the dead which die in the Lord from henceforth: Yea, saith the Spirit, that they may rest from their labors; and their works do follow them" (Revelation 14:13). Larimore did, however, live long enough to see much good results from his school and his "boys." The congregation at Mars Hill owes him much gratitude, because of his influence almost at the beginning back at much gratitude. Larimore may have saved the Mars Hill congregation through his quick thinking to purchase the old foundry property and prevent a brewery from being built on the doorsteps of his school, which was about to be launched. Through this purchase, the church could have a large building in which to worship and grow. They used this old foundry shop until 1904 when their new house was completed.

For their annual meeting in 1894 Larimore's brother-in-law—R. P. Meeks came and helped him in the meeting. A. B. Simpson of Waverly, Tennessee wrote concerning this meeting:

> Brother Meeks will go to Mars Hill, Ala., to join Brother Larimore in a meeting. Where could be found a stronger team? May the Lord bless them, together? with the brotherhood. A. B. Simpson. *Gospel Advocate* (August 2, 1894): 486.

Three weeks later the *Gospel Advocate* published a final report on the Mars Hill meeting:

> Mars Hill, August 17. Brother Meeks' meeting at Mars Hill added eleven to the fold-just eleven more than we

expected, material being so scarce that additions were scarcely to be expected. Material never accumulates about Mars Hill. *Gospel Advocate* (August 30, 1894): 550.

Mars Hill was saddened again in September 1894, when another of the Mars Hill family was "promoted to eternal life." One of the John A. Thompson family's children died. The following was printed in the *Gospel Advocate*:

Miller Chisholm Thompson was born at Mars' Hill, Ala., July 25, 1868, where he obeyed the gospel. July 21, 1888; where, in the house in which he was born, his final farewell to this world, he said (on) Jan. 13, 1894. Miller was the tenth member of the family to which he belonged, and the tenth to pass away; father, mother. Mollie, Maggie, Minnie, Florence, Romie, Johnnie, and Jimmie having gone to the grave before he left us. Mollie and Maggie were taken from the cradle. "Of such is the kingdom of heaven." The others were all members of the Church of Christ—the family of God. Robert, still living at the old home, with his faithful Christian wife and three little children, is the only surviving member of the large and happy family dwelling there a few brief years ago. Thus, generations pass away, homes are vacated, and graveyards are filled! He who writes, and those who read this, "like shadows are flitting away." How are we living? Whither are we tending? Our bodies are going to the grave. Whither are we going? Let us live to do good for God shall bring every work into judgment.

with every secret thing, *Gospel Advocate* (September 27, 1894): 611.

The way this report was written, it seems to have T. B. Larimore's touch of the pen. Whoever it was, they had firsthand knowledge of the Mars Hill family and also, the Thompson family.

Two years later the last living son of John A. Thompson died. The following obituary recorded a short sketch of his life:

Robert Henry Thompson was born at Mars' Hill, Ala., Oct. 19, 1859. He was "born again" at the same place Feb. 13, 1876. He was married to Miss Erin Augusta Owen Dec. 28, 1886. On Feb. 13, 1896-the day between the day of his death and the day of his burial, just twenty years after his burial "by baptism into death" with Christ-his lifeless body was tenderly and tearfully prepared by loving hands, in the same house in which he was born, for burial in the Mars' Hill cemetery. Robert was the last of a family of eleven to obey the solemn summons that comes to all the sons and daughters of men-father, mother, three brothers, and five sisters having "gone before." All were Christians, except two precious little baby sisters—Mary and Margaret—who went home to Him who says, "Of such is the kingdom of heaven," when father and mother were young. One family less, where life is "a vapor that appeareth for a little time, and then vanisheth away." One family more, "where life is eternal, and a treasure sublime."—T. B. Larimore. Florence, Ala. *Gospel Advocate* (April 2, 1896): 215.

John A. Thompson was Larimore's brother-in-law and had been a strong supporter of the Mars Hill work—both the school when it was operating and the Mars Hill Church.

Larimore began a meeting at Mars Hill in 1897 but had to shorten it because of ill health. He wrote of it:

> It grieves me not to be able to preach as these perfect days are going by. I baptized three gentlemen in Florence last night but was not able to preach. I am to go to Lawrenceburg tomorrow, but my judgment and friends here tell me to quit trying to preach and try to get well. We had eleven confessions at Mars' Hill, but I had to close the meeting in the midst of the best interest we have ever had here. Aug. 14, 1897. T. B. Larimore. *Gospel Advocate* (August 26, 1897): 530.

Larimore continued to hold meetings at Mars Hill each August. He held one in 1898 while still very exhausted and sick. F. D. Srygley wrote of his condition:

> Brother Larimore spent the night of May 23 at my home on his way from Springfield, Mo., where he had just closed a meeting, to his home at Mars Hill, near Florence, Ala. He was in feeble health, and in his body bore the marks of serious exhaustion from overwork when he ought to have been resting and recuperating his nervous system and general health ... —F. D. Srygley. *Gospel Advocate* (June 30, 1898) 406.

Srygley wrote again in September of that year concerning Larimore's health and his work at Mars Hill:

The latest news from Brother Larimore is encouraging. His health is steadily improving, and he hopes to be able to resume regular work as an evangelist by the first of September. For several years he has held an annual protracted meeting at his home, Mars' Hill, Ala., in August of each year. These meetings have always been well attended by people from a distance as well as by the neighbor around Mars' Hill. The interest from a distance has for some years attracted the attention of railroad authorities, and special excursion rates have been given to Mars' Hill during Brother Larimore's annual protracted meetings. The congregation this year was probably the largest that ever assembled there. The house though large for a country congregation, would not hold the women; and if it had been four times as large, it would have been packed. Brother Larimore preached twice on Sunday and expressed the opinion next day that he would be all right and ready for regular work again by the first of September. If a prophet is always without honor in his own country, then Brother Larimore is certainly no prophet. He has more honor, and he draws larger congregations at his own home, where he has been heard most and known longest and best, than anywhere else F. D. Srygley. *Gospel Advocate* (September 1, 1898): 549.

In October Strother M. Cook, a missionary to Africa, came and solicited funds for his work abroad. Since Mars Hill was so mission minded, we believe that they contributed to his work. He wrote:

> At the present time I am among some of the churches in North Alabama. The churches at Florence, Mars' Hill, Sheffield, Russellville, Bear Creek, Haleyville, Buttahatchie, Lynn, and Jasper have been visited and most of them have' given cheerfully to our mission ... *Gospel Advocate* (October 6, 1898): 640.

Mars Hill demonstrated time and time again their concern for mission work, both at home and foreign. Perhaps this was no exception.

Little information between 1898 until 1903 can be found in the journal. 1903 was a mixed year for Larimore and Mars Hill. Larimore's son Theophilus Brown Larimore, Jr., better known around Mars Hill as "Toppie" died August 4, 1903. G. C. Brewer gave an account of this sad story:

> On August 4, 1903, death invaded for the first time the home of Brother Larimore. His son, Theophilus (tenderly called "Toppie") passed away. He was an osteopathic physician, thirty-one years old, and had his office at Winchester, Tenn. From childhood he had been a cripple. He suffered with what used to be called "white swelling," but which is tuberculosis of the bone. When the final fatal attack seized him, his mother went to Winchester and brought him home to Mars Hill. The family physician, Dr. Bramlette, said an operation was necessary. Arrangements were made to take him to Nashville to Dr. Eve. The Louisville and Nashville Railroad runs by Mars Hill, about one mile from the Larimore home. This railroad company had arranged a stop and built a small station booth

there for Brother Larimore and called it "Mars Hill." Automobiles were unknown, and such a thing as an ambulance did not exist in that section then. But good neighbors were in abundance, and kindness and love were the law of the community. Neighbor men, with "Toppie's" brothers, carried him on a cot to the train; and when they came to the Creek, spanned by a one-person foot log, they waded it without hesitation. "Toppie" and Brother Larimore reached Nashville safely, and the operation was performed successfully. Brother Larimore had already written a telegram of hope for the loved ones at home, when a sudden change came, and death was almost immediate. "Toppie" was brought home and buried at Mars Hill on Thursday. The following Sunday, August 9, the annual meeting began. Brother Larimore was so overwhelmed with sorrow that he feared he could not preach. The brethren talked of getting someone else, but no one seemed to be available on so short a notice, and Brother Larimore, looking to the Lord for strength, agreed to go on with the usual plans. He preached with a deeper pathos and a more compelling tenderness because of the bleeding heart that throbbed in his bosom.—G. C. Brewer. *Gospel Advocate* (February 15, 1940): 147.

During the death of "Toppie" there was much sadness at Mars Hill. Emma Page wrote a tribute to Toppie in the *Gospel Advocate*:

The time of the annual meeting at Mars' Hill (usually in August) is reunion time for Brother Larimore's family. The children who have left the home nest always come back then if possible. Toppie had never failed to be at one of these meetings. Thirty Augusts he had seen come and go; thirty of these memorable meetings he had attended. Even when he was just recovering from his long spell of suffering and sickness, —unable to walk, he was carried to the meetings, where propped up in a chair, he enjoyed the services as much as anyone else and contributed his share to the general happiness. The meeting this year began on August 9—five days after Toppie passed away, and three days after his burial. It was a sad meeting for Mars Hill family, especially for the father and the mother, who missed the bright face of their son who had never failed to be with them at their reunion time, always happy and cheerful, always doing everything in his power to add to the happiness of others— many little things which no one else seemed to think of doing. *Gospel Advocate* (December 24, 1903): 819.

For some time talk around the Mars Hill church had been concerning the condition of the old shop in which the church had been meeting, since they left the old Hopewell building. In 1903 Mrs. Horace P. Lucas, who was a member at Mars Hill, took it upon herself to send an appeal to the brotherhood concerning helping build a new meeting house at Mars Hill. Since the appeal was the catalyst for getting things in motion for the new building, we give the appeal in full:

Mars' Hill, Ala., four miles from Florence, Ala., is the home of our beloved brother, T. B. Larimore. While nearly all of the people of that community are members of the congregation of Christians worshiping there, there is no wealth in the congregation, because there is none in the community.

Florence is my home now; but my membership is still at Mars' Hill, where I was born and brought up and where Brother Larimore baptized me when I was a little child.

While Brother Larimore and the members of the congregation at Mars' Hill have helped many others in many places and in many ways, always trying to respond to every call for help, we have necessarily denied ourselves, that we might help others, which, of course, it was our duty to do. One result of this is that we worship in what was once a blacksmith shop, now nearly fifty years old.

Now we are not ashamed of the dear old shop, the sacred memories and sweet influences of which are felt in ten thousand homes that have been made better, brighter, and happier thereby; but we have resolved that, the Lord willing, Brother Larimore shall have a better house in which to preach, and his friends a better house in which to hear him, when he is at home. We know that there ought to be, and we believe that there are, thousands of grateful, faithful friends who will be glad to contribute liberally to this important work (who, indeed, would sincerely regret not having an opportunity to do so); and to all such the privilege is now, once for all, extended.

Brethren, to all who really appreciate the privilege of giving not grudgingly, but gladly and literally little or much to this important work we appeal for help, and to no one else. We will build the best house that we can build; we will build it this year; we will pay as we go, owing nothing when the work is completed; and we will be careful to put into it not even so much as one penny, farthing, or mite that is not a freewill offering —a love offering, gladly given. Therefore, if you really wish to help us, please do so now. You shall not be worried by a repetition of this appeal. If you help us, we shall be grateful, and may the Lord bless you; but if you refuse to respond to this appeal, you reject the only opportunity that you will ever have to help us. It is now or never. We want no pledge or promise; we want cash. and nothing but cash, as we shall plan and build according to the cash on hand, contracting no debt. So, then, "what thou doest. do quickly;" and may the Lord abundantly bless you.

Please send all offerings to Mrs. Horace P. Lucas, 'Miss Ettie Larimore. or Mr. L. C. Moore, Florence, Ala., or T. B. Larimore, 900 South College Street, Nashville, Tenn.

(Mrs.) Horace P. Lucas. Florence, Ala. Brethren D. C. M. Southall, W. H. Gresham. J. B. White, H.C. Blalock, and L. C. Moore indorse the foregoing statement and appeal, as follows: "We, the elders of the churches of Christ at Florence and Mars' Hill, commend Sister Lucas as worthy of all confidence, love, and esteem; we approve and appreciate her unselfish labor of love; and we direct and request that the foregoing important, worthy, and righteous appeal be published by order of the churches that we represent." (A Flyer titled "An Appeal," *Gospel Advocate* (August 30, 1903): 285.

The new building was no longer just a dream. By November it was under construction, according to a report in the *Gospel Advocate*:

> Work has begun on the new house of worship at Mars' Hill, Ala. A few days ago Brother Larimore preached the last sermon in the old shop which has done such useful service. Brother Larimore is now in a meeting with the Tenth Street church of Christ, this city [Nashville]. *Gospel Advocate* (November 5, 1903): 709.

In 1904 Sister Lucas requested Larimore to make a statement through the pages of the Advocate, concerning the former appeal, which he reluctantly wrote. We also give his statement in full:

> Sister Lucas, who recently resolved to build a memorial meetinghouse at Mars' Hill, (my home), insists upon my submitting to my friends, for her a statement, that the situation and the status of the work may be better understood by all interested or concerned.
>
> As Chicago, Nashville, and St. Louis all postponed their great expositions one year because of not being ready on time, so, while our memorial meetinghouse, of much more importance to us than all of those combined, was to have been built this year, it is to be built next year—is to be completed, seated, and made perfectly ready for service in time for our annual protracted meeting in 1904. So many friends expressed regret that it was to be built before they could contribute to it as they desired that duty

seemed to demand this delay, that none might be thus disappointed. Now all who will, can help.

Sister Lucas wishes me to state that all contributions, great or small, will be gladly and gratefully received till the work is done; that every penny received will be appreciated and shall be properly applied; that she is anxious for every one of my friends to contribute something to the work.

That nothing but freewill, love offerings is desired, that no tricks, traps, or schemes or shows shall be resorted to in order to raise a dollar; that the house shall be for service, not for show; that it shall contain nothing that any conscientious Christian cannot recognize as right; and that absolutely no debt shall shadow it when work and worship begin therein. She wishes me to also state that, while she hopes all our friends may manifest an interest in our work, she herein and hereby request some true friend in every community reached by this call to make a careful canvass of the community and write to friends in the interest of the work.

Contributions may be sent to Mrs. Horace P. Lucas, Miss Ettie Larimore, or Mr. L. C. Moore, Florence, Ala., or T. B. Larimore, 900 South College Street, Nashville, Tenn. Now having submitted the statement that Sister Lucas requested me to submit, I wish to say of my own volition and on my own responsibility, that she, whom I have known all my (her) life, who was my pupil in school, whom I baptized when she was a little child, is worthy of all confidence, love. and esteem. No sinister motive prompts her to do anything that she does. She seeks no notoriety, praise, or position, and would not under any circumstances, accept a penny for the labor of love she is performing. She longs to see the work accomplished. because of the good it will do; and it is the dream and desire of her heart that every friend I have on earth shall contribute something to it. When she first mentioned the matter to me, I protested earnestly against it; but she insisted. and said: "Your friends all love you; you love them and want to please and bless them; it will be a sweet pleasure; and a great blessing to them to build the house, and they will gladly build it."— T. B. Larimore. *Gospel Advocate* (September 3, 1903): 575.

The building was finished in late summer of 1904, just in time for the annual meeting at Mars Hill. The new building was the talk of the town as can be seen in the *Florence Times* report:

"Big Meeting At Mars Hill. First Services Held In New Christian Church."

The new Christian church at Mars Hill was opened for service for the first time Sunday, when Elder T. B. Larimore preached to two large audiences morning and afternoon.

Much interest was manifested in the meeting, people coming from far and near and listening with the closest attention to the eloquent sermons of the distinguished preacher.

A basket dinner was spread on the grounds and many hundreds of people enjoyed a royal feast.

The meeting will continue until August 28,

services being held at 10 a.m. and 8 p.m. on weekdays and at 11 a.m. and 8 p.m. on Sunday.

The music will be in the charge of Dr. I. K. Harding of Bowling Green, Ky., who assisted at the recent meeting at the Christian church in Florence, assisted by John T. Glenn of Nashville.

There were two additions at the Sunday services. The church building is a modern structure and entirely out of debt, the last cent of indebtedness having paid off. *Florence Times* (August 15, 1904).

Sister Lucas' dream of having the building paid in full by the time of the meeting was realized, as can be seen in the Florence Times report.

Larimore's brother-in-law, J. C. Ott kept a diary religiously and wrote of the first meeting in the new building. He wrote:

Sun. 14—I went to church at Mars Hill. Bro. Larimore preached for the first meeting in the new church.

Mon. 15—I went to town and returned and hauled a load of hay.

Tues. 16—I went to church at 10 a.m. Hauled two loads of hay in afternoon.—J. C. Ott, *Diary*, (August 1904).

We next hear from a report on a meeting held by James A. Harding at Mars Hill in 1905. During this meeting, E. G. Prosser was baptized. The following account sums up Prosser's Christian life:

> He obeyed the gospel under the teaching of James A. Harding at Mars Hill in 1905, being baptized at "The Bluff," in the creek that flows by the peaceful meeting place where T. B. Larimore preached and taught for many years. Brother Prosser gave himself to the cause of Christ from that time until his death. On June 3, 1908, he married Loudie Moore. *Gospel Advocate* (May 22, 1952): 341.

Harding holds the honor of being the first outside preacher to hold a meeting in the new house of worship at Mars Hill. Before, it had been local men—after Larimore spoke in the first meeting.

In a report from Corinth, Mississippi we read of contributions from Mars Hill to Corinth brethren's building fund. It read as follows:

> I acknowledge the receipt of contributions to the fund for building a house at Corinth in which we, the disciples of Christ, may worship as the New Testament directs: From the Mars' Hill Church, through Sister Stinburger, $10; Brother C. M. Southall, $2; Brother H. P. Lucas, $2.50; by Sister Stinburger, 50 cents ...—T. M. Darnall. *Gospel Advocate* (August 30, 1906): 338.

This report revealed members who were interested in good works to help other good work in other places.

The next year—1907 turned out to be a sad year at the Mars Hill congregation—it seemed to be the year of death. In March Larimore's wife Esther died from extended illness. J. C. McQuiddy, a Larimore Boy, wrote of Esther's death:

> Sister Larimore died early Monday morning, the 4th inst., and was buried at the family burying ground at Mars' Hill at three o'clock Tuesday afternoon. Thus, a noble mother in Israel has fallen. She was a woman of firm convictions, sunshiny nature, and one who wielded a great influence for the cause of truth. She ably assisted her husband in the great work which he did at Mars' Hill for seventeen years. When it was thought best to discontinue the school, she stayed at home and thus made it possible for her husband to do the great work he had done in the field. The influence of her life will be far-reaching. A large crowd attended the funeral, which was conducted by Brethren Meeks and Elam and me. *Gospel Advocate* (March 14, 1907): 169.

Then in July, Emma Page authored a memorial essay about Esther Larimore:

> Sister Larimore—Julia Esther Gresham—was born, on July 11, 1845; "born again"—born into God's family—October 21, 1859; married, to T. B. Larimore, August 30, 1868; went home, March 4, 1907. This is a brief record of a life filled to overflowing with the fruits of the Spirit—a life that shall live in the memory of those it blessed as long as they shall live and live in the fruits of its influence forever. She grew to womanhood in the house in which she was born, Florence, Ala; spent most of the years of her married life in sight of

her girlhood home; and her body sleeps in the family burying ground near that same peaceful, country home. Her life, however, near Mars' Hill, was not circumscribed by narrow bounds. Her sphere of usefulness was broad, her influence, far-reaching.

F. D. Srygley, one of the Mars Hill students, wrote of her, in his first book, *Larimore and His Boys*, the following tribute to the mistress and "mother" of Mars' Hill:

She is dignified in bearing, kind in manner, calm under trying circumstances, firm in her convictions, constant in her affections and patient in hope. She has the fortitude of a martyr, but she is neither fanatical nor excitable by nature. She is forever at work, and an incessant singer. She sings over the cook stove, sings while arranging the dining room, sings in the nursery, sings at the sowing machine, sings in the garden-wherever she goes she sings and works with an earnestness that defies penury: and mocks despondency. "As a mother, wife, Christian, she is the equal of the best-an honor to Christ and a blessing to his cause"-is the estimate a distinguished man who knows her well has expressed of her. In formulating and carrying out practical business plans, she is an invaluable assistant of her distinguished husband, In this line she is peculiarly well adapted, both by natural gifts and early training, to be a true helpmate for him.—F. B. Srygley, *Larimore and His Boys*, Nashville: Gospel Advocate Pub., 221).

F. B. Srygley dearly loved the Larimore family. T. B. Larimore was his idol and mentor. He loved his memories of Mars Hill. He had observed the Christians at Mars Hill and was always remembering their influence upon his life.

In October Larimore reported the death of another faithful Mars Hill woman. She was Mattie Price Moore, an enthusiastic worker for Christ. She was constantly concerned with the cause of Christ and the church of God at Mars' Hill. She worked for Christ for a third of a century. She was one of the loyal, faithful, and true who went home from that historic Christian home of Christian workers in 1907. Larimore wrote:

> Sister Moore (nee Miss Mattie Price) was born in Lauderdale County, Ala., where she lived all her life, May 8, 1844. She was married to L. C. Moore, February 28, 1867. She was not a charter member of the Mars' Hill congregation, but became a member thereof shortly after its establishment, and was a willing, worthy worker therein from the day on which she was "born again" till Heaven called her home. *Gospel Advocate* (October 24, 1907): 685.

Like Esther Larimore, she was one of the very earliest members of the church at Mars Hill.

On November 11, 1908, Louis S. Blalock and Irma Griffith were married at Mars Hill. T. B. Larimore officiated the ceremony. (Marriage license). This was a happy event and was not reported in the *Gospel Advocate*. Larimore was traveling very often that year and must not have had the time to send a report on the wedding. He usually reported such an event.

We know very little about the church at Mars Hill from 1908 until 1911. Our only reference to the church was a report on support sent by members of Mars Hill to the Tennessee Orphans Home:

> L. C. Moore, Mars' Hill, Ala., $2; Miss Maggie Gresham, Mars' Hill, Ala., 50 cents; W. H. Gresham, Mars' Hill, Ala., 50 cents; G. N. Daugherty, Mars' Hill, Ala., $1; Herschell Larimore and wife, Mars' Hill, Ala., $1.50. *Gospel Advocate* (November 9, 1911): 1302.

Two years later Isaac C. Hoskins wrote about his association with Mars Hill. He gave an insight into Larimore's work there. The following article reads as follows:

> Florence, Ala., July 7.—Brother T. B. Larimore has been telling "the wondrous story" at Mars' Hill with characteristic pathos, sweetness, and power. The meeting began on the second Lord's day in July and closed on the third Lord's day, with three sermons both Sundays and two each day between. Six were immersed and one restored. The meetings were well attended-immense crowds on Sundays-and the interest fine. It has been five years since I heard Brother Larimore, and it was exceedingly gratifying to note how well he looks (though suffering from an ailment that will quickly pass, I think) and how forcefully he preaches the word. As I preach once a month at Mars' Hill, there was, in addition to the pleasure of

hearing Brother Larimore, the added pleasure of meeting these dear friends; and it will be a great pleasure, if the Lord permit, to have this godly man back again next year to " preach the word " at Mars' Hill.— Isaac C. Hoskins. *Gospel Advocate* (July 31, 1913): 733.

The next to the final report on the Mars Hill church came in October of 1914. It was a short, to-the-point report as follows:

David Lipscomb Cooper, Fisherville, Ky., August 30 to September 13, fourteen baptisms, two from the Baptists, two restorations, six by letter; Mars' Hill, Ala., September 20-30, five additions, two restorations. *Gospel Advocate* (October 8, 1914): 1060.

J. Paul Kimbrell gives a report on his work in Lauderdale County in which he mentions going to Mars Hill during a meeting and hearing Brother Cooper preach a sermon:

While in Florence, I went out to Jacksonburg, where Brother Hoskins was holding a meeting, and heard him deliver a sermon. Before returning on Monday, I drove out to Mars' Hill, in company with Brother W. G. Wallace, of Rogersville, and listened to a sermon by Brother Cooper, of Kentucky. Yesterday (the first Lord's day in October) I began a series of meetings at the Bradley School house, in the southern part of Wayne County. Large crowds were present at both services. I am expecting some results, as there is plenty of material to work on. After the meeting closes, I will go back to my home at West Point and will probably enter school after Christmas.—J. Paul Kimbrell. Iron City, Tenn. *Gospel Advocate* (October 22, 1914): 1110.

The Bradley school mentioned above was a congregation established by J. R. Bradley at his brother Andrew Jackson Bradley's school.

J. R. Bradley visited Mars Hill in the fall of 1916 and preached at the Church at Mars Hill. He gave a good report on his visit:

> I preached (or tried) three times—Saturday night, Sunday and Sunday night—to fair audiences in a splendid house of worship which stands on the very spot where the Bible Hall stood, in which we "boys" read, studied, and debated the things pertaining to the kingdom of God and the name of Jesus Christ. I certainly felt, very sensibly, that schoolboy embarrassment which I used to have to suffer in making speeches and in trying to preach in the presence of Brother Larimore. I did certainly wish for him there to take my place, if he would, but glad that he was not present if I had to try to preach. I could not help, even while in the pulpit, thinking of not only Brother Larimore, but Sister Larimore also, and her sweet and melodious voice in singing the praises of God. Precious to us all was the "Mother of Mars' Hill" *Gospel Advocate* (November 16, 1916): 1149.

Imagine the excitement that raced through J. R.'s mind when he arrived at his old school grounds. You can feel the emotional rush he must have felt on that occasion. This was his last trip to the Florence area. He died in 1923.

W. S. Long made his first preaching trip to Mars Hill for the annual August meeting in August 1917. Long reported on the progress of the meeting at Mars Hill on August 21:

> I am now in a meeting at Mars' Hill. One has made the good confession and been baptized and the interest is good. Let us pray for good meetings and more laborers. *Gospel Adovate* (August 30, 1917): 844.

He then sent a follow-up report on the meeting on September 4. It stated:

> Manchester, September 4.—The meeting at Mars' Hill, Ala., closed on August 30, with sixteen additions —eleven baptized and five restored. In every way it was a pleasant meeting and, in many ways, a successful one. Many happy hearts gathered to greet each other and spread dinners and suppers on the beautiful lawn around the church house. Many happy faces greeted each other. The one that impressed me most was the face of our faithful brother and "father in Israel," W. H. Gresham, who is eighty-six years old. It did me good to know of his godly -life and to hear his trembling voice in earnest prayer to God. The memory of that meeting will be a joy to me. Thanks to the thoughtful hands that administered to encourage the meeting. We have some excellent brethren and sisters there who will push the work to a successful standard.

May God's blessing be upon them, and may, the church be a model church, like the one we read of in the Bible.—W. S. Long, Jr. *Gospel Advocate* (September 13, 1917,): 904.

Shortly after this meeting, Brother W. H. Gresham passed to his eternal reward. On November 14, 1917, Brother Gresham answered the call that all men must answer—the call of the grave. He had been a pillar of the church and community for decades. Mars Hill lost an irreplaceable member.

Long returned in 1918 for another meeting. He described the congregation colorfully in the following report:

From W. S. Long, Jackson, Tenn., August 22: "I have just closed a very interesting meeting at Mars' Hill near Florence, Ala. The meeting was well attended both day and night. A. C. Traylor led the song service and did his part well. There were six baptisms and one restoration. I preached one night at Jacksonburg. Ala., and two were restored and one baptized. As I had to go to another meeting, Brother Traylor continued the meeting. I love to labor with the Mars' Hill church, because they love the cause of Christ and spare no means to make the meetings a success. My home was with the Gresham family. This is the home of our beloved W. H. Gresham (brother-in-law of Brother Larimore). who passed to his reward last February. This is one of the happiest homes I have ever been in, and they know how to take care of a preacher so he may be able to do his best. May the Mars' Hill congregation be a burning and shining light till the end of time. I am to begin a meeting at Cottage Grove. Tenn., next Sunday." *Gospel Advocate* (August 29, 1918): 825.

From the meeting Long held in 1917 forward the Mars Hill church developed a bond with Brother Long and began to aid him in his mission work, as is established in this short report below:

Work in Washington by W.S. Long, Jr. Church at Mars' Hill, Ala., gave $38.55 ... *Gospel Advocate* (February 6, 1919): 141.

Larimore came back for possibly his last visit to the Florence area. Due to declining health, he was restricted in his travels. The following report was his last report on the Mars Hill work. We give the report in full:

Mars' Hill, August 11-Yesterday was the first day of our annual Mars' Hill meeting—the first one I have attended in six years—and it seemed to be entirely satisfactory. We had a large all-day attendance, with preaching morning, afternoon, and night. "Egypt" (the old Wade community) was well represented, as was the whole country within a radius of twenty miles of Mars' Hill. Many of the old Mars' Hill pupils, their children and grandchildren, were there. So, you see, the audience was composed largely of my children and grandchildren in that sense, and several of my children and grandchildren in a literal sense were there. Then there were old-time friends with their children and grandchildren there. Hence, it was really a great reunion. I am preaching as I have been preaching more than fifty years—twice every day and three times each Sunday. Services begin each Sunday at eleven, three, and eight-thirty; each week day, at three-thirty and eight-thirty. —T. B. Larimore. *Gospel Advocate* (August 21, 1919): 820.

It turned out that that meeting was the last meeting he held at Mars Hill. This was confirmed to E. H. Ijams and J. M. Powell by Virgil Larimore when they visited him in March 1950. *Gospel Advocate* (April 28, 1960): 258. In October of that year, one of the last charter members passed away. She was the last of the original members of the Gresham family. Larimore wrote of her in a lengthy obituary:

Miss Maggie E. Gresham was born at or near Mars' Hill, Lauderdale County, Ala., Wednesday, December 11, 1839, hence would have been fourscore years old, if she had lived till December 11, 1919; but she passed away, Tuesday, October 28, 1919.

She was born, baptized, and buried where she lived all the years of her busy, useful life; hence, where the sweetly solemn summons found her, perfectly prepared to go, when the call came. No final preparation was necessary then.

Sister Maggie obeyed the gospel when she was a sweet little girl, and thenceforth lived as she believed she ought to live till she reached the end of life, doing as wisely and well as she could whatsoever, she believed duty demanded. She was a Christian nearly threescore years and ten, and Christ and his cause were always first with her ... *Gospel Advocate* (January 29, 1920): 120.

From 1920 until 1937 the *Gospel Advocate* and other brotherhood journals were silent of the congregation at Mars Hill. In September of 1937, the silence was finally broken. In retrospect—meetings for 1935 and 1936 had occurred; but not reported in any paper. We learn that John D. Cox had held meetings in the two previous years at Mars Hill. He wrote:

John D. Cox, Charleston, Miss., August 27: "I have conducted meetings at Ford's Well, near Oakland, Miss., with no additions; and at Mars Hill, near Florence, Ala., with six baptisms. This was my third meeting in succession at Mars Hill. H. Leo Boles begins our meeting September 5." *Gospel Advocate* (September 2, 1937): 832.

G. C. Brewer held a meeting at Mars Hill in August 1939. He wrote a lengthy report on his visit:

Mars Hill. The meeting at this place was announced in the *Gospel Advocate* and also through some other papers before it began. The second Sunday in August has been the date for this meeting for more than a half century. We began on schedule, and many visitors were there the first day of the meeting. All the congregations in that section of the country had made announcements of our meeting. C. C. Burns, who conducts a radio service for the whole Muscle Shoals area, had announced the meeting, and he attended it as often as his time would allow.

Chester Estes had announced the meeting in his paper, which is published at Corinth, Miss., and the brethren at Mars Hill had advertised in the local secular papers. The first day of the meeting visitors were there from Fort Worth, Texas; Memphis, Tenn.; Lawrenceburg, Tenn.; Sheffield, Tuscumbia, Florence, Russellville, Jasper, and possibly other towns of Alabama. On the second Sunday people were there again from all these places except Fort Worth, Texas, and from several additional places—among them, Paducah, Ky.; Nashville, Tenn.; and Huntsville and Decatur, Ala. We had three sermons on each of these Lord's day days, and there was a bountiful spread at the noon hour. The few brethren that compose the congregation at Mars Hill brought enough food by themselves to feed the entire crowd. The meeting continued for one week only, and six grown persons were baptized in the beautiful, clear stream of water—Cox's Creek—which flows through the grounds of Mars Hill and forms a beautiful natural baptistery nearby. The place where Brother Larimore baptized in the long ago is at the foot of the bluff, which is Mars Hill proper, and which bluff rises with a solid rock face several feet above the stream. The floods have so changed this place that it is not now suitable for baptizing. We were only a few feet removed, however, from the same spot as we baptized penitent souls this year. *Gospel Advocate* (October 19, 1939): 986.

Grover Cleaveland Brewer held the meeting at Mars Hill in August 1940. He gave a full summary of what to expect at the Mars Hill meeting:

> At this writing (July 15) I am preaching in the city park at Whitesboro, Texas. Bill Davis, of Dallas, is conducting the singing. He is a fine young man and a splendid singer. From here I will go to Midland, Texas, to assist C. C. Morgan and the church there in a meeting. From Midland I will go to Mars Hill, Ala., for the annual meeting. Brother Larimore's meetings at this place always began on the second Lord's day in August. The church keeps up the custom. The date this year is August 11-18. Let our readers take notice of this date, and all who can come should arrange to attend the meeting.
>
> There will, as always, be dinner on the ground and three sermons on each of the two Lord's days. The nearby churches are hereby requested to announce the afternoon services. If the house will not accommodate the Lord's-day-afternoon crowds, we will speak out in the beautiful, shady church yard. Bring a basket and come for the whole day. The Mars Hill congregation is small, and we should not expect those few families to feed all the crowd. Bring a basket and spread with us as in the good old days.
>
> From dear old Mars Hill I hope to gain inspiration for the rest of the year's hard schedule. Address E. Gaston Collins, now at Lubbock, Texas. Mail addressed to me there will be promptly forwarded. *Gospel Advocate* (July 25, 1940): 713.

Upon the remembrance of a little-known incident that happened at Mars Hill, G. C. Brewer wrote further of the meeting he held at Mars Hill in August 1940:

> Forty years, almost to a day, from the time Brother Larimore was relating the above story we will be conducting the annual meeting at Mars Hill, the scene of the story. The meeting begins on August 11 and closes the 18th; lasts only one week. Come and worship with us and walk over the grounds that were long ago hallowed by these scenes of sorrow and love, of faith and victory. *Gospel Advocate* (February 29, 1940): 202.

Three years later in July 1944, Virgil Larimore announced the upcoming August meeting at Mars Hill. It was to be held by G. C. Brewer. Brewer was a local boy who grew up in East Florence and who had become a renowned preacher throughout the brotherhood. Larimore wrote the following about why the meeting was held in August:

> In accordance with a long-fixed custom, the annual eight-day meeting at Mars Hill will begin the second Sunday in August, with G. C. Brewer, of Lubbock, Texas, preaching. Dinner will be served on the grounds each Sunday between the morning and afternoon services. We hope many of the friends of Brother Brewer and those of the Mars Hill congregation may be able to be with us at many of the services. *Gospel Advocate* (July 27, 1944): 502.

Kenneth B. Adams of Huntington, W. Va., came and held a gospel meeting from August 10 through August 17, 1947. He wrote:

> This was the home of the beloved T. B. Larimore and the site of Mars Hill College, which he established and conducted for several years. Many preachers and others from the Muscle Shoals area attended, and the song services were led by Brother Hibbets, of Poplar Street Church, in Florence, and Brother Walters, of Mars Hill. *Gospel Advocate* (August 28, 1947): 665.

Sometime after this meeting a Brother Keaster came and labored with this congregation. Julia Buffler, a lifelong member wrote a short history for the Mars Hill church:

> In 1947 Brother Keaster came and we started Sunday night and Wednesday night services. He was here for a short time (approximately two years). When he left, Paul Simon came and we have had a regular preacher from then on. (An unpublished document written by Julia Buffler, in the Mars Hill papers, no date).

Paul Simon came to work on a regular basis with Mars Hill Bible School and the Mars Hill congregation in September 1949. Simon wrote on March 10:

> I have assisted in twelve meetings during 1949, with ninety-one baptisms, one hundred-five confessions of sins, and five others came from the Christian Church. Five have been baptized into the Mars Hill congrega-

tion since my coming last September. *Gospel Advocate* (March 23, 1950): 184.

Paul Simon's reports were basically about the meetings and baptisms. We give his short statements about the work at Mars Hill. His first report:

Paul Simon, Mars Hill Bible School, Florence, Ala., July 28: "The meeting in Shillington, Pa., was unusual in several respects. Among those baptized was a Catholic, a Seventh Day Adventist, a Lutheran, and a Dunkard. Two Baptist women were baptized at Mars Hill last Sunday. I am in a meeting at Morristown, Tenn., and will begin at Ramer, Ala., August 7." *Gospel Advocate* (August 10, 1950): 514.

A. R. Hill, Sr. (father of Albert Hill) preached at Mars Hill on July 9, 1950. This would have been during the time Paul Simon was away holding a meeting in Shillington, Pennsylvania. *Gospel Advocate* (August 10, 1950): 514; (August 31, 1950): 560.

A.R. Hill, Route 5, Florence, Ala., August 21: "I preached at the following places during July: July 2, Killen, Ala.; July 9, Mars Hill, Florence, Ala.; July 16, Lawrenceburg, Tenn.; July 23 and 30, East Florence, Ala. I assisted in a vacation Bible school at Weeden Heights, Florence, Ala., July 10-14." *Gospel Advocate* (August 31, 1950): 560.

The remainder of Simon's reports are given below:

Paul Simon, Mars Hill Bible School, Florence, Ala., November 8: "H. A. Dixon. President of Freed-Hardeman College assisted us in a meeting at Mars Hill in August. Attendance was unusual, interest was excellent and the preaching was of the best. There were no additions. F. B. Shepherd, of Sweetwater, Texas, preached each morning for us at school for two weeks in October. There were eight baptisms and one restoration." *Gospel Advocate* (November 29, 1951): 762.

Following this report comes a very brief one in 1952 stating:

Five were baptized at Mars Hill during March. *Gospel Advocate* (April 24, 1952): 267.

A. R. Hill reported that he had preached at Mars Hill, probably in August, since his report was published on September 7, 1953. *Gospel Advocate* (October 1, 1953): 643.

In July B. C. Goodpasture announced on July 14, that he was to hold a meeting at Mars Hill. *Gospel Advocate* (July 22, 1954): 576. J. E. Thornberry of Shepherdsville, Kentucky came to Mars Hill and visited with Virgil Larimore for a week. While there he preached some. He described his visit in the report below:

J. E. Thornberry, Shepherdsville, Ky., July 20: "I have just returned from Mars Hill, Ala., where I spent a week in the home of Brother and Sister A. V. Larimore. Brother Larimore is the youngest son of our departed brother, T. B. Larimore. While there I preached five times and visited many homes, During the thirty-five years I was located in Lawrenceburg, Tenn., I usually preached once a month at Mars Hill and since I have returned to my old home in Kentucky I visit them at least once a year. The church is in a prosperous condition. Paul Simon, president of Mars Hill Bible School, is their minister. B. C, Goodpasture will conduct their meeting July 25—August 1." *Gospel Advocate* (July 29, 1954): 596.

Apparently Goodpasture came and held the meeting, but no report was ever found on the results. It is interesting that Simon never reported anything on that meeting either. At this time Simon seemed to be making preparations to leave Mars Hill. This is apparent in the following report by Simon:

Paul Simon, Route 6, Box 46, Florence, Ala., October 29: "Mars Hill Church and Stony Point Church supported me to the amounts of $100 and $50 per month during the summer while doing evangelist work in Maine ... I have resigned all connection with Mars Hill Bible School and am now devoting full time with the church. Six have been baptized at Mars Hill recently." *Gospel Advocate* (November 25, 1954): 941.

Paul Simon gave a report in which he announced that he was leaving Mars Hill to take a work in Henderson, Tennessee. We have inserted his report in full:

Paul Simon, 235 Second Street, Henderson, Tenn., March 10: "I have just closed five years and six months with the church at Mars Hill, Florence, Ala. During this time fifty-eight were baptized, fifteen of which were baptized in February, and eighty-four confessed faults. I also taught in Mars Hill Bible School for two years, served as president for three years, and conducted forty-five meetings, in which one hundred forty-seven were baptized. I began work with the church here on March 1." *Gospel Advocate* (April 14, 1955): 298.

Mars Hill aided in getting a functioning student center at Alabama Polytechnic Institute (Auburn). C. W. Whitten wrote a report on this endeavor:

C. W. Whitten, 137 Toomer Street, Auburn, Ala., May 20: "In February of this year Max Hughes came to work as an assistant with the church in Auburn devoting his time largely to the students in Alabama Polytechnic Institute here. Assistance on his support is being provided by congregations at Hartselle, Housh Chapel or Fayette, Kingville, Luverne, Mars Hill of Florence, Oliver of Lexington and West End of Birmingham, besides Auburn's part in this need. Individuals have also aided. Two hundred eighty-five students here are either members, married to members, or indicate the church as their religious preference. Brother Hughes teaches classes each week, does personal work among the students, and assists them in planning desirable Christian fellowship and recreation." *Gospel Advocate* (June 9, 1955): 473.

Besides doing domestic and foreign mission work,

the Mars Hill church-supported educational works such as the one at Auburn and even at the University of North Alabama.

The congregation was blessed to be in an area where many good gospel preachers lived. They were ready at a beckoned call to fill the pulpit at Mars Hill when the local preacher was away. A. E. Emmons, Jr. was one such man. He reported a Sunday meeting at Mars Hill:

> A. E. Emmons, Jr., Box 37, Mayfield, Ky., June 18: "On June 12 I preached at the Mars Hill Church in Lauderdale County, Ala., and one was baptized. Crawford Allen is their local evangelist." *Gospel Advocate* (July 11, 1957): 443.

Byron Davis was the local minister at Mars Hill from 1958 until March 1960. He sent a report about the work:

> Byron Davis, 803 Humes Avenue, North east, Huntsville, Ala., March 21: "I began work with the East Huntsville Church March 20. I was with the Mars Hill Church in Florence for two years. During our stay in Florence fifty were added to the congregation, a preacher 's home was built and a heating and cooling plant was installed in the meetinghouse. Recently four elders were appointed at East Huntsville." *Gospel Advocate* (April 14, 1960): 234.

By June Mars Hill had hired Robert M. Waller as their minister. Waller wasted no time in reporting on his new work:

Robert M. Waller, Mars Hill Road, Route 6, Florence, Ala., June 13: "After four and one-half years in Dongola, Ill., I have begun work with the Mars Hill Church. July 3–13 I will assist in a vacation Bible school and do the preaching in a meeting at Fountain Head, Tenn." *Gospel Advocate* (June 30, 1960,): 410.

About six months he sent a second report:

Robert M. Waller, Mars Hill Road, Route 6, Florence, Ala., December 1: "Recently two were baptized. The old Mars Hill meetinghouse now has new floor tile and tinted walls. A library for church use and a private study is nearing completion at the preacher's home. We are helping to spread the gospel in several different places." *Gospel Advocate* (January 5, 1961): 12.

From this report, we learn about some face-lifting with the old meetinghouse. Waller seemed more interested in mission work than the local work. Most of his reports were about mission work. It seemed that his heart was very much with mission work, and it was good that Mars Hill was pleased to encourage him in that endeavor. His next report bore this sentiment also:

Robert M. Waller, Route 1, Mars Hill Road, Florence, Ala., July 13: "Four were baptized and one restored in our recent meeting and vacation Bible school at Fountain Head, Tenn. Greer Hendon, their minister, did a fine job of directing the song service. Our meeting at Mars Hill with H. A. Dixon will be August 5–12. My next meeting will be at Villa Hills, Ill." *Gospel Advocate* (August 9, 1962): 509.

No further report concerning the Dixon Meeting ever graced the pages of the *Gospel Advocate*.

Maurice Howell wrote that he would hold the annual meeting at Mars Hill for the year 1963:

Maurice M. Howell, 335 Mockingbird Lane, Port Arthur, Texas, July 24: "During June I conducted a meeting with the Foote Street congregation, Corinth, Miss. Nine were baptized. We worked with this congregation from 1942 to 1947. I was also with the congregation in Friendship, Tenn., in a meeting. My next meeting will be with the Mars Hill church, Florence, Ala., July 28–August 4." *Gospel Advocate* (August 15, 1963): 525.

Waller gave a report on Mars Hill of results for the Howell meeting:

Robert M. Waller, Route 1, Florence, Ala., August 31: "At Mars Hill two were baptized during our meeting with Maurice Howell. The church has started a building fund and a weekly radio program on WOWL. During my meeting at Harrisburg, Ill., three were baptized." *Gospel Advocate* (September 19, 1963): 606.

Next Waller announces that he is leaving the work at Mars Hill:

Robert M. Waller, Route 1, Box 66, Florence, Ala., May 18: "We are closing six years of enjoyable and profitable work with the Mars Hill church. June 1 our new address will be Rt. 2, Box 2-A, Princeton, Ky. 42445. There is only one church in the county. Worship with us if you are vacationing in the Kentucky or Barkley Dam area." *Gospel Advocate* (June 2, 1966): 349.

In 1969 a new house of worship was built and according to Julia Buffler, the congregation moved into the new building in 1970. In 1999 a fellowship hall was built onto the main building. (An Unpublished document written by Julia Buffler, in the Mars Hill papers, no date).

The last report in the *Gospel Advocate* was published in December 1971.It was by Glann M. Lee. It contained very little information—simply that he held a meeting at Mars Hill during 1971. *Gospel Advocate* (December 2, 1971): 769.

The following year a report partially pertaining to the church at Mars Hill appears in the *Gospel Advocate*. It was the obituary of a key member at Mars Hill—Virgil Larimore. We summarize Hill's article:

Andrew Virgil Larimore (sometimes known as A. V. or Virgil), son of the late T. B. and Esther Gresham Larimore passed away on December 31, 1972. Brother Larimore was born February 3, 1879, and was the last of the direct descendants of the T. B. Larimore family. He was born, lived, and died near Florence, Alabama. He was a member of the Mars Hill congregation where he served for many years as a deacon. His funeral was conducted at the Mars Hill church building by Kenneth Davis and Larry Gooch. His body was laid to rest in the Florence Cemetery. *Gospel Advocate* (February 8, 1973): 90.

This concludes our chronological history of the first-century Mars Hill Church of Christ. We leave the rest of Mars Hill's history to others who desire to preserve it.

An Article

T. B. LARIMORE

※

Mrs. Mattie Price Moore, an enthusiastic worker for Christ and his cause in the church of God at Mars' Hill, Alabama, a third of a century, is one of the loyal, faithful and true who have gone home from that historic, Christian home of Christian works this year.

Sister Moore—née Miss Mattie Price—was born, in Lauderdale County, Alabama, where she lived all her life, May 8, 1844. She was married, to L. C. Moore, February 28, 1867. She was not a charter member of the Mars' Hill congregation; but became a member thereof shortly after its establishment, and was a willing, worthy worker therein from the day on which she was "born again" till heaven called her home.

Having proper conceptions of the importance of salvation eternal, and being devoted to her husband and children, their obedience to the faith filled up her cup of happiness to over-flowing. Probably the one event that gave her more genuine joy than any other was the obedience of her husband. He, before he obeyed the gospel, as he has been ever since, was a model man, neighbor, citizen, friend, husband, and father, with as clear a record as Cornelius ever had; but his faithful, worthy wife was a model Christian several years before he became obedient to the faith. When he did obey, her cup of joy was full.

Our sister was the mother of twelve children: six boys and six girls, eight of whom survive her. She buried four babies—all boys. She lived to see her eight children grown, four of them married, and each of them a Christian—except one son—her beloved baby boy—and we hope he may not defer his obedience long.

Thirty years ago, Sister Moore's trusted and trustworthy physician, having spent two or three consecutive days and nights in her home, earnestly endeavoring to save her life, abandoned all hope and left here, saying as he left the house: "She can't live twenty minutes"—also subsequently saying, when told that she was still alive, "I know that cannot be true. I hurried away from her yesterday, to keep from seeing her die. I know she's not alive today." Many then pupils at Mars' Hill remember that eventful, sorrowful, joyful day; and many who have never seen Mars' Hill have read, in the book, *Larimore and His Boys*, the thrilling story of Sister Moore's marvelous faith manifested then and there. The calmness with which our beloved sister virtually met death that day and the joy with which she anticipated the happy meeting "over there" can never be forgotten by the thoughtful who were there.

Mrs. Moore and Mrs. Larimore—"Mattie" and "Esther," they called each other—were close, confidential friends. Both slowly but surely slipping away from us at the same time, they visited each other as long as they could. The last time I saw Sister Moore, which was only a few days before she went away, she said, "Tell Esther I'm coming to see her just as soon as I can climb the steps. I couldn't climb those steps now to save my life." When I delivered the message, Mrs. Larimore said, "Yes, I know she'd come to see me if she could."

Sister Moore went home February 6: Mrs. Larimore, March 4—1907—the saddest year Mars' Hill has ever known.

T. B. Larimore

Reminiscences of Mars Hill Church of Christ

AN INTERVIEW

KENNETH DAVIS INTERVIEWING MR. VIRGIL LARIMORE

Every generation that lives upon this earth is deeply blessed by those who have gone before. The age in which we live is no exception. We enjoy thousands of blessings every day that were unknown to those who lived before us. We warm by fires we did not build. We plant upon ground we did not clear, and we worship in buildings built by the toil of countless others of days gone by. For all these things were should be truly grateful. We cannot be properly grateful of today unless we understand yesterday.

Given below is an interview that was held with brother Larimore a few weeks ago. It was mechanically recorded and is given here as it was recorded. This material is rather general in nature and we hope to give a fuller account later on with the help of brother Larimore and others who may be willing to help. We appreciate very much the willingness of brother Larimore to help in the compiling of this material. K.D. (Kenneth Davis)

In order to simplify matters the letter "Q" is used to indicate a question. "A" indicates the answer given by brother Larimore.

Q. When did the congregation start here at Mars Hill?

A. Well, I think it started when my father came here and started the school in the first of January, 1871.

Q. Is the building that we have now the original one?

A. O' no, this building was built in 1904.

Q. Could you tell us about those responsible for its being built?

A. It was built by the Mars Hill congregation, but we had donations from various places, students, old students at school here made donations. It wasn't done altogether by the Mars Hill congregation as far as the financing was concerned.

Q. Was brother T. B. Larimore working with the congregation at this time?

A. He never preached regularly for the congregation here but now during school days maybe he did, but I don't remember that, that was before my time. I was never old enough to go to school to him.

Q. Were the classrooms built along with the rest of the building in 1904?

A. No sir, the auditorium was all we had until-well-I don't remember, but I would say fifteen years ago there were two classrooms built and a baptistry put in and the restrooms, but I don't have the dates on that.

Q. Who originally owned the land on which the building stands today?

A. Well, far enough back, I reckon would be my father. He bought it just after the school started from Governor Patton.

Q. Who were some of the early preachers here at Mars Hill?

A. We only had preaching at the big meeting times, we called it, the protracted meeting in the summer. Brother James A. Harding and of course later brother H.A. Dixon, brother Brigance who taught for so long at Freed-Hardeman (College), and brother (Maurice) Howell has held two meeting for us.

Q. Do you remember any outstanding meetings in which there were very large crowds?

A. Yes, the L & N Railroad, through the influence of brother Stribling of Lawrenceburg, I imagine, ran a train from Summertown down here and unloaded every Sunday of the big meeting and the people just swarmed —like the house wouldn't anything like hold them. I've seen my father stand there and preach with children sitting all around the pulpit just as thick as they could sit—he just had them under his feet.

Q. Could you tell us about the services in those days? How long did the preacher preach?

A. Way back there preachers usually preached an hour ... sometimes an hour and a quarter but our regular services were just Sunday School, we don't have a preacher very often, except at protracting meeting time.

Q. Could you tell us anything of a general nature regarding the church here?

A. Well, our congregation here at one time got mighty weak and through brother Finley it kept from just going out. Brother Finley kept it going, and he was the father of the Miss Ann Finley who goes to church here now. Brother Finley and his wife, of course his wife helped him, kept it going. Brother Finley was baptized by brother James A. Harding when he held a meeting down here.

Q. Have many people been baptized in the creek down here near the building?

A. Yes, my father baptized there for years. Brother Howell baptized 20 some-odd, 26, I believe in a meeting that was held up here at the Bible school.

Q. Thinking back just a minute—is the present building located a the same place as the original one?

A. Yes, but at a different angle. The old building was not designed as a church house. It was just part of the old foundry building. The front end of it, which. was the blacksmith shop, they tell me was converted into a chapel for the school and we used that as our church building from the time the school was organized in 1871 until 1904.

The visions and dreams of yesteryear are ever with us. They are manifested in the things which we see about us and in the lives of those who heard the word of God and obeyed. For all these things then we are grateful but we realize that with these blessings also come responsibilities. Those of days gone by carried out their responsibilities to God by seeking to plant in this community the "kingdom which shall never be destroyed." May we live and work in such a way that in the ages to come men may say of us—"they were faithful too."

History of Mars Hill Church of Christ

Every generation that lives upon this earth is deeply blessed by those who have gone before. The age in which we live is no exception. We enjoy thousands of blessings everyday that were unknown to those who lived before us. We warm by fires we did not build. We plant upon ground that we did not clear, and we worship in buildings built by the toil of countless others of days gone by. For all these things we should be truly grateful. We cannot be properly grateful for today unless we understand yesterday.

The Mars Hill congregation has indeed been blessed with a rich history. The congregation's beginning closely parallels that of the school which Brother T. B. Larimore stated in the Mars Hill community before the turn of the century. The congregation first developed a chapel in one part of a foundry that existed on the current property with worship services conducted there. Brother Larimore frequently preached for the congregation during the school year but was usually away in meetings during the summers. The old building was constructed in 1904 because it was felt that a preacher of Brother Larimore's statue should have a proper place to preach. After Brother Larimore left the area, the congregation continued meeting through the influence of the Finley, Moore, and Blalock families. Usually, they met for Bible study and had the communion service. Visiting preachers spoke when they were in the area.

The building in current use was constructed in 1969. Men who have served as ministers through the years are Paul Simon, Byron Davis, Robert Waller, Kenneth Davis, and Randy Baker. Those currently serving as elders are Howard Ivey, Delbert Knight, Henry Ligon, Cris Moore, and James Swinea. Current deacons are Clif Hinton, Ray Horsman, Pat Ligon, Henry Miles, Danny Rickard, and James Riedout.

Through the years this congregation has been strongly involved in mission work in many areas of the world. Presently, we provide the support for the Jerry Tackitt family in Georgetown, Kentucky; Fred Dillon for his work among the elderly; Harold Gilmore at Moulton Heights in Decatur; the Student Center at the University of North Alabama; the foreign works include Brother Don Waggoner's work in Indonesia, the work in Korea, work in the Caribbean and involvement with the World Bible School in Nigeria.

Benevolent involvement outside of the local efforts includes support for orphan homes and Lauderdale Christian Nursing Home. The congregation repeatedly responds when there is a national emergency, such as a hurricane, where there is an opportunity to demonstrate that Christianity is not deaf to the needs of those round about us.

Unknown author and date

My Tenure at Mars Hill

RANDY BAKER

It was my privilege to serve as the minister of the Mars Hill congregation for 17 years, and my family will always consider that as our home congregation. It was a blessing to my family and the great members there were a positive influence on all four of our children. Both our daughters were married there and one of the boys was married on the grounds of the Larimore home.

There was one event that occurred while I was preaching at Mars Hill that has never occurred at any other congregation where I served as minister ... one Sunday morning as I concluded my lesson and stepped down from the pulpit, I noticed something on the carpet a little green snake and my immediate thought was, "Somebody is playing a trick on me just to see how I would respond." It was at that point that the little fellow wiggled and I knew he was real. Brother Ray Horsman was sitting near the front and he may have seen the expression on my face that tipped him off, but as soon as the "amen" was said, he swung into action with a songbook and took care of the unwelcome visitor. I've heard of dogs meandering down the aisle in days gone by, but I have yet to hear of another preacher who had a literal snake come forward during the invitation.

A Church that Began Because of Harrasement

JACK WILHELM

In the early 1860s harassment by Union soldiers played a part in the religious heritage of the Mars Hill community that no one at the time could have predicted. During the war, some families, especially Gresham and Thompson, in the Mars Hill community north of Florence were walking or traveling by wagon to worship in the Cypress Creek community, near where the Stony Point Church of Christ now meets. The Union soldiers camped along the road often stopped them as they went back and forth, to search their wagons and be sure they were not assisting Confederates. Due to the harassment, the families decided to begin meeting in their homes. They continued to meet in the community after the War Between the States ended.

The present Mars Hill Church of Christ and Mars Hill Bible School grew out of influence that began as Christian families met in a chapel in one part of an old foundry. The foundry had been used to make cannonballs during the war.

T. B. Larimore married Esther Gresham and settled in the community about 1870. He began Mars Hill Academy in 1871 and operated it until 1887. At one time, several buildings were on the campus, on the same site where Mars Hill Bible School has operated since 1947. Many ministers and church leaders received training. Lairmore would preach for the Mars Hill church while conducting his school from January to June each year. Then he would travel and conduct religious meetings nationally for the other six months. His longest meeting lasted nearly six months in Sherman, Texas with 3 lessons daily.

Because of growth, the Mars Hill church built a nice building in 1904. It has been maintained and is still used for singings, weddings, and special services. It has been recently repainted, and some landscaping and sidewalks have been added, along with a wheelchair ramp to make it more accessible. Air conditioning and some carpeting were added also.

Larimore eventually moved to California where he died in 1929, but his influence on many families in the community is still felt. The Finley, Moore, and Blalock families were largely responsible for keeping the congregation meeting through the years. They would always meet for Bible study and communion, but often visiting preachers spoke when they were in the area.

The present main building of the congregation was built in. 1969. A new annex was added in 1999. All of the buildings are well-maintained in a beautiful wooded setting of grass and shrubs that is accentuated by an enchanting creek that flows through the property. The present minister, Jack Wilhelm, recently set out some ivy near the old building that has an unusual pedigree. He has the ivy growing at his home, and it came to him from the garden of John Vaughan in Columbia, Tennessee. John had gotten it from his father, who in turn had gotten it from the gardens of J. M. Powell and David Lipscomb. It reportedly had come to them from the garden of the Scottish poet, Robert Burns.

Besides T. B. Larimore, other ministers who have served the church are Paul Simon, Byron Davis, Robert Waller, Kenneth Davis, Larry Gooch, Randy Baker, and Tim Grigsby. In addition to Wilhelm, Bill Bagents serves as an associate minister and John Paul Heupel works with the youth and leads singing. Other ministers attending the congregation are Basil Overton, Fred Dillon, and Malcolm Glover. Five former members have recently begun preaching regularly for other congregations.

Men currently serving as elders are Lawrence Alexander, who has always attended the congregation since childhood, and Homer Ray Horsman, Delbert Knight, and Hobert May. Deacons are Bill Bagents, Jimmy Beadle, Rickey Collum, Randy Medley, Tim Morrow, Brant Young, and John Zahnd.

The congregation has been deeply involved in mission work, locally and worldwide. The church directs the program "Televisit With the Bible" which began in September 1957. It is seen daily at 1:30 p.m. on UPN 15. A number of members have a special interest in mission projects in addition to what is done through the church treasury. The church meets at 1330 Mars Hill Road in Florence.

Mars Hill Is Added to Alabama Register

The original Mars Hill Church of Christ, located on Rt. 11, Florence has been reviewed and added to the Alabama Register of Landmarks and Heritage.

L.C. Moore, an elder of the Mars Hill Church, prepared the information for review by the Alabama Historical Commission.

"The main block of the building is rectangular, measuring 30 feet by 60 feet," Moore said. "A foyer measuring 7 feet by 10 feet abuts the facade and has a hipped roof with a roofline lower than that of the main block.

According to Mr. Moore, the church, a simple single-story frame building typical of many rural churches in Alabama, still stands on the original site.

"The church is well maintained and is not significantly altered," Moore said.

Moore gives the following background of the church:

AN EARLY HISTORY OF THE MARS HILL CHURCH OF CHRIS...

Mars Hill Church of Christ was built in 1904 through the efforts of T.B. Larimore, a nationally known Church of Christ minister, and is located near his home. The congregation was organized by Larimore, who at one time operated a school in the area to train Church of Christ ministers, and for a time he served as minister in the building.

Following the Civil War, Larimore's work as a minister brought him from Tennessee to North Alabama where he married and settled. The school he opened in 1871, known as Mars Hill College and later as Mars Hill Academy operated six months of the year until 1887.

Following the close of Larimore's school in 1887, he lived in his home until 1907. He left the area several years later. In 1946, the home was bought by a non-profit corporation for educational purposes. Lauderdale County Bible School began in the home in 1947. Its name was changed to Mars Hill Bible School in 1951, and it has operated continuously since its organization.

Mars Hill Church of Christ still serves the community, although regular services are no longer held there.

It is used occasionally for weddings and social events.

The Alabama Register is a prestigious listing of historic, architectural, and archaeological landmarks.

A Letter

NELSON SPARKS

5-30-04
Jack Wilhelm and Bill Bagents

In response to your statement in regards to our homecoming.

Eva and I were not at Mars Hill church at its early years, but we came back to Florence in August of 1989, and have been a part of the Mars Hill family beginning about 1992.

I remember many of the people who encouraged us to be a part of the church here, Cris and Dell Moore, Basil and Margie Overton, Sonny and Margaret Miles, Sanders Blalock, James and Flo Hopper, Bebe and James Swinea, Henry Ligon and Randy Baker to name a few.

We feel as if we have been a part of the congregation a long time. It is always an inspiration to have an activity in the old building. I'm glad we have it.

Brother Cris used to tell of the time he got up early Sunday morning and went to the building and built a fire in the old pot belly stove or heater.

I think of some of the old path preachers that probably preached there—T. B. Larimore and many others.

We are proud to be a part of the family at Mars Hill.

The many missions of the church at Mars Hills excel above many who have a much larger membership, and that is a great compliment to our elders and members as well.

I just want to express to you and Bill our love for Mars Hill and also to you and Bill.

Sincerely and in Christian love,

Nelson Sparks (and Eva)

Mars Hill Church Memories

JULIA BUFFLER

―

The first memories I have of the Mars Hill Church were when I was very young since I have been going there from the time I was a baby. Of course, it was in the old building that was built in 1904. When you entered the door, you would see stoves in the front of the building, one on each side near the front.

There were oil lamps hanging from the ceiling. To be filled, cleaned, and lit someone had to get a ladder to do this. The only times these lamps were used was during the two-week meetings that always began the second Sunday in August. That was when we had night services.

I remember the Lord's Supper table in the center at the front of the auditorium. It had a white starched cloth on the table with two cups and a pitcher. They were silver, and the bread was served from two silver plates. The bread was homemade by some of the members.

The juice was put in the cups and passed from

person to person, each one drinking from the same cup. This usually took place at the end of the service. The collection was taken during the last song. We did not have a song leader; I guess there was not a man who could lead. So one of the women would start the song while seated.

We did not have a preacher for a long time. so one of the men would read a scripture and make some comments. We just had Sunday School. Most of the time there were two classrooms, used by the "card class" and the "paper class." The other classes were in different parts of the auditorium and you can imagine trying to listen to your teacher when the other classes were talking at the same time.

Later we had preaching on the 3rd and 5th Sundays. Brother Thornberry came from Lawrenceburg on the 3rd Sunday. He would stay and have lunch with some of the members and preach in the afternoon at Kilburn Church, and then go home. We did not have a night service. He was a good preacher. He would usually preach an hour and some of the younger people would get fidgety. Brother Coffman came from Lawrenceburg, too, and he usually went home after the morning service. He usually didn't preach more than 30 minutes. He said, "Know what you are going to say, get up and say it and sit down."

In 1947 Brother [James C.] Keaster came and we started having Sunday night and Wednesday night services. He was here for a short time. When he left, Paul Simon came and we have had a regular preacher from then on.

At about this time, four classrooms, and a baptistery

were added. Prior to this, baptisms were in the creek below where the Lewis home is now. In cold weather, we had to go to one of the churches in Florence.

We would have a meeting each year with a visiting preacher, beginning the 2nd Sunday in August for at least a week. On Sundays during the meeting, we would have dinner on the ground—and I do mean on the ground! The women would spread table cloths on the ground. I just wonder how they managed to get down to put the food out, but you should have seen all the good fried chicken, sandwiches and apple pies and cakes and all the trimmings.

We had to take our drinking water, as there was no running water except the creek. After eating, everyone would have to make a trip to the spring, which was on the other side of the creek. There was a swinging bridge you could cross or else cross by stepping on the rocks, but when you got to the spring, it was worth it, as it was good and cool. The spring was just below where the Lewises now live. Later, some of the men built tables to spread the dinner on. This made it more convenient.

During these meetings, we had three sermons on Sunday. One was at 2:00 o'clock, after lunch. Then we would go home and come back for night services. During the week there would be two services, one either in the morning or afternoon and another at night. Usually, the visiting preacher stayed at some of the members' homes and different families would have him for meals during the week. Some of the outstanding peachers we had for meetings were: T. B. Larimore, L. L. Brigance, bro. Harding, G. C. Brewer, John Cox, H.

A. Dixon, Basil Overton, Leon Burns, Charles Chumley, and many more.

The road used to go on the other side of the church building and there was no bridge, so you had to ford the creek. You had to really be careful or you would get in to deep water.

We moved into the new church building in 1970. We had a kitchen and small fellowship room. We now have a new, larger fellowship room, which was built in 1999, that accommodates the entire congregation and visitors.

{This article includes some of the highlights I referred to last Sunday, June 6 2004.—jw (Jack Wilhelm)}

Our History

RION GOLDEN

The history of Mars Hill church of Christ is a long and interesting one. The church has run continuously since being established in 1871 by a group of Christian men and women previously worshipping at the Stoney Point community.

Throughout the mid-1800s, individuals from the Mars Hill community would travel to Stoney Point to worship. During the Civil War, Union soldiers captured the road between the two communities and would inspect the wagons of all who were traveling the road, harassing those traveling to worship; the congregation couldn't continue traveling to Stoney Point. They decided to meet in an old foundry used to make cannonballs for the South. The foundry was located near the current church location. Brother T. B. Larimore began preaching for the congregation, though he was never a full-time pulpit preacher because he was gone so often preaching at meetings. He was essential in the survival of the congregation during its early years.

The church continued meeting in the foundry until 1903 when they had simply outgrown the small chapel. Brother Larimore and several others in the congregation helped to buy the land for the new building. The congregation then built a new church building (the old building on the current Mars Hill church campus) which was ready for use in 1904. The church then began having regular services there.

The church would continue to worship there until 1969 when the current build was completed. Over the years, the Mars Hill church would have several wonderful men preaching God's word. These were: T. B. Larimore, Paul Simon, Kenneth Bryon Davis, Robert Waller, Kenneth Odell Davis (no relation to Kenneth Byron Davis), Larry Gooch, Randy Baker, Jack Wilhelm, and Cory Collins. The congregation currently has two wonderful men serving as the pulpit preachers: Chris Moran and Bill Bagents. They also have a youth minister, four elders, and four deacons proudly serving the Lord. The church now has over 150 regular members, many of whom have attended the church for years. The long, rich history of Mars Hill has spanned over many years—and looks to continue for many more.

Included in the 2019 Church Directory.

Memories

I'm 4th generation to attend Mars Hill. My great-grandparents on my mother's side and father's side went to Mars Hill and along with great aunts and uncles and others helped build the old building.

My great-grandfather set out the old maple trees around the old building.

The "big" meeting went from Sunday to Sunday and each Sunday had "dinner on the ground." There were long tables set up and filled with food. Each lady would bring "her specialty." One time I remember Leo and Irene Womble would have cantaloupe sliced really thin in a bigmouth two-gallon jar. There would be all kinds of meat, vegetables, deviled eggs, and sandwiches that would sit in cars all morning during service, and then be put out to eat. Don't remember anyone getting sick.

There was an eight-day clock hanging on the right side over the "amen corner." Every Sunday morning before Sunday school Virgil Larimore, T.B. Larimore's son, would stand on a bench and wind it. When he got where he couldn't stand on the bench Cris Moore took over that duty. When it was quiet that clock could be heard ticking even in the "vestibule."

Communion treys were on the table in front covered with a white linen cloth which was ironed before each Sunday. The men who presided over the Lord's supper had to fold it just so.

Belle Walker, from across the creek, was my Sunday school teacher when I was little. each week we had little 5x7 inch sheets of paper with our lesson on one side and a Biblical picture on the other.

After Belle Walker and I "moved up" my mother taught the younger children. She built a sandbox to be a visual aid (it's still in one of the classrooms).

Sanders Blalock (my cousin) had a horse named Lazarus. Many Sundays during the summer he rode from St. Florian to church and tied the horse to a tree next to the spring behind the building.

When the new building was built, Kenneth Newton (Denise Golden's father) built the levy along the creek to prevent it from flooding the building. Katherine Walker, from across the creek gave orders not to let bulldozer even one inch on their side of the creek. She watched constantly to see it didn't happen.

Mary Hazel Jones has attended Mars Hill all of her 96 years. She was baptized in the creek when she was young.

The old building had two wood or coal-burning stoves in front and the windows swung out in the summer —nobody had air conditioning at that time but don't remember being extremely hot. There were lots more maple trees at that time and were sheltered all day long. In the fall the young people got together and raked leaves.

When the new building was built in 1969 we had almost 200 attending in the old building on Sunday mornings and 130-150 on Wednesday nights.

Mack Blalock

Just thinking about when we were children at the old Mars Hill church building. We couldn't wait for church to be over to play and jump off the huge millstone in front of the church. Some of the braver ones jumped off the ledge of the steps and Daddy would catch them. This would go on and on as long as the adults were fellowshipping in the front yard. Is the millstone still there?

I doubt if there are many left who remember the "Dinner on the Grounds." Maybe Lawrence A[lexander]. and Ann Ligon. The Mars Hill women were the best cooks in the world. I would give anything for a piece of Mrs. Ona Moore's apple pie. The crusts were soft and the apples almost like homemade applesauce. She stacked them in layers of about three or four pies and cut down through all of them, but that slice would be served to three or four people if you can envision that. Her great-granddaughter Patsy Harris and I tried to come up with a recipe last fall but fell way short.

Don't know if you're looking for little silly stories or not, but I thought of a couple .... The Alexanders had a large family, I think 6 children. They lived on Chisholm

Road by the farmer's market. They didn't count the kids as they left church one Sunday and they left Lawrence behind. He came up and asked Daddy if he was going by his house on the way home. Daddy thought it was so funny because he of course lived on Mars Hill Road in the opposite direction. Daddy loved Lawrence all his life and of course Polly too.

Velma Moore (later Tays and Mike Tays' mother) taught the little kids' class in a room at the rear of the building. I think those rooms were demolished when the new church building was built. Anyway, my little sister Ellen was in her class. She had been of course teaching them all the things little ones need to know and this particular Sunday she emphasized prayer. She asked my sister, now what's the last thing you say before you go to bed? Ellen replied, "Mama, get the Vicks. My nose is stopped up!" I'm sure that wasn't the only funny thing Vea heard in her class.

We teenagers were sitting close to the back. Some of the boys started causing a little commotion that night. I can't remember if Daddy came after me or if he and Mother just looked back at me with an evil eye. What they learned after church was that a wasp or two had come in the open windows and Eugene Bennet was trying to dodge them. Of course, we were all giggling. I don't know why that didn't happen often!

Another funny time Daddy came in late and sat down putting his arm up on the bench around Mother. The only problem was it wasn't Mother. It was Bessie Mae Smelser. Everyone behind them was in stitches.

They told this story on me, but I was too young to remember. I was a bed wetter for most of my younger life. Uncle Virgle Larimore was my great uncle and always sat on the front row because he led our singing. I loved to go down front to sit with him. Big mistake!! I went to sleep one Sunday night and wet the bench. When he stood up to lead the invitation song, his trousers were wet. I don't think they let me sit with him anymore. I'm sure he was glad of that.

They took me to Poplar Street Church, which later became Wood Ave. because I responded at night. I said that I wished I had responded during the morning service so I could have been baptized in the creek. Mother had stayed home that night with my baby brother who is eleven years younger. I remember it was quite a stir going to get her. No cell phones of course back then. She was a little hurt I believe, but somehow I had worked up the nerve that night.

Martha Jane Harrison

I remember Sanders Blalock riding his horse to church every Sunday and tying it out front.

Robert Roberson and family came every Sunday with mules and a wagon. They would sit on the front row. The two boys would go to sleep with their heads back and sleep the whole service.

Windows opens in the summertime. Bugs everywhere. One night a lady sitting down front had a July fly get up her dress. She hollered all the way to the back and outside until she got it out.

There used to be a lot of trees around the building.

One night during a thunderstorm, lightning struck a tree out front as we were coming out after service. It ran down the handrail coming down the front steps and hit a woman; she hollered but it did not kill her.

Cris Moore used to catch me jumping off the steps.

We had big dinners on the ground. During meetings in the summer, Momma would fix tea or lemonade and tea with a log of sugar in a 5-gallon lard bucket. It was good!

I remember people would park everywhere. All the roads were gravel; none were paved.

Cris Moore would come early to church during the winter and start a fire in the potbellied stove.

Church would last one to two hours.

We had a lot of visiting preachers.

Many of the children were barefooted.

My parents left me at church one day. I asked Cris Moore if he was going my way and would drop me off.

Lawrence Alexander

I remember sitting on wooden pews with my family. The big windows open during the summer.

We would play on the big round rock that was out front of the building. There would be dinners on the ground under the trees (not on the ground).

Going on hayrides. We would climb into the back of a big farm truck filled with hay and ride to a park and grill over a fire.

Listening to Bro. Waller.

Wondering who the amen corners were for.

I remember being served grape Kool-Aid and sugar cookies at Vacation Bible School.

Denise Golden

The classrooms were in the back of the building and I remember Mrs. Keiffer was my Sunday school teacher.

I remember the windows would be open during the summer.

When I was baptized we had to go to Sherrod Avenue because there was no baptistery in the old building.

When I married my husband, Pat, we were married in the old building.

Ann Ligon

I remember getting stung by a wasp because they used to open the windows in the summer.

We played chase after church and that millstone was base.

I remember Virgil Larimore singing bass (guess that aged me pretty bad).

If you had to go to the bathroom during church you had to walk toward the front.

A former member

I remember the men stoking the fires in the old black stoves for heat in the winter. In the summer they opened the windows and used very tall fans that rotated. One summer night, the windows were open and a large moth flew in and went right down the front of a lady's dress. She stood up and started screaming, jumping, and "dancing" around to get the moth out. It was quite a scene and although I was a young child, I remember wondering if she would have to go to live with the devil because she danced in church.

The classes were held in rooms located at the back of the building (No longer there). I loved going to Sunday School classes especially when we used the sandbox, flannel boards, and other visual aids. We had a lot of kids and their families who attended.

I remember us playing on the old rock water wheel after church.

The acoustics in the old building are still. fantastic. The wooden ceiling helps with the beautiful singing. The simple leaded glass windows from Germany are still mostly intact, even today in 2024. This well-preserved building is a jewel in our community and is still used for singings, weddings, funerals, graduations, and other special events.

Judy Young

In 1957 we moved to North Florence. As a young couple with a small child (Ed age 2), we were blessed to have as our new neighbors Clif & Wadean Hinton, who were faithful members of Mars Hill Church of Christ.

Soon we were invited to attend services with them. We did and found our forever church home.

I was baptized in 1958 by Byron Davis. As I grew spiritually, I began teaching the 2-year-old class, which I did for the next 50 years. Ed loved to go to his class and was excited each Sunday to get to his class.

In one sad memory, Ed was learning not to talk during worship. One Sunday, I told him if he talked again, I was going to take him out., it happened, I picked him up and went out, falling down the front steps with him. We never had to go out again.

In March 1961, our son Steve was born, and six weeks later Hobert was baptized by Robert Waller. That was a very special day for our family.

The sweetest memory was Steve as a 2-year-old would like to stand on the pew and keep time with our song leader Howard Lewis. I was going to make him sit down, but Bro Howard said you let him stand up and lead singing, he will be a song leader one day. He was right, Steve has been leading singing in Mobile for the past 42 years.

As we all grew to love the Lord, we had so many happy memories, wonderful teachers to teach us, and good elders to lead us. We were so blessed our boys grew up with so many who loved and encouraged them along the way to be the Christian men, they are today.

When Hobert passed away in 2012, I could not have handled it without God and our loving and caring family at Mars Hill. My family has so many wonderful memories of the past and is still making memories today with all my Mars Hill family.

Willodean May

I remember going to class in rooms at the rear of the building. Cards when we were young and later, we had the quarterly books (I think from Gospel Advocate) you had to get your lesson every week.

I remember the meetings every August that went from Sunday through the next Sunday. Bro. Hibbett from Poplar St. usually led the singing. "Dinner on the ground" or really plank tables was a big, delicious meal. We had three services on Sunday then afternoon services and night services during the week.

We lived right below Beechwood on Mars Hill Road. Mother and I would walk to the day service. One day I told Mother before we went that I was going to be baptized. I remember we were sitting on the left ½ way down when I responded. I was baptized in the creek. Bro. Irvin Lee was holding the meeting.

Later as teenagers, we had a vast number of young folks, and Bros. Cox and Morris saw to it that we had hayrides, wiener roasts, and short trips. Most of us went to Mars Hill Bible School and saw each other six days a week. We gathered under the trees after services and sang for a while.

I remember the wood stoves and open windows and bugs flying in.

Fond memories, good memories, and blessed to have grown up at Mars Hill!

Edith Daugherty Broadfoot

Enrollment

1. E. Gresham IIIIIIIIIIIIIIIIIIIIII
2. B. Larimore IIIIIIIIIIIIIIIIIIIIII
3. Hattie J. Young IIIIIIIIIIIIIIIIIII
4. J. Bates IIIIIIIIIIIIIIII
5. Joonna Brooks IIIIII
6. Brattie Breenam IIIIII
7. Minnie Braty IIIIIIIIIIIIIIII
8. Sallie C. Braty IIII
9. Belle Gresham IIIIIIIIIIIIIIIIIII
10. Ella E. Parkhill IIIIIIIIIIIIIIIIIIII
11. Mary A. Gresham IIIIIIIII
12. Bettie D. Gresham IIIIIIIIIIII
13. Maggie L. Gresham IIIIIIII
14. Mary D. Larimore IIIIIIIIIIIII
15. Lizzie M. Thomkson IIIIIIIIIIIIIIII
16. Rebecca Wade IIIIIIIIIIII
17. Emma J. Carter IIIIIIIIIIIIIIII

. . .

1. Parkhill IIIIIIIIIIIII
2. Young IIIIIIIIIIIIII
3. Braty IIIIIIIIIIIIIIIII
4. L. H. Dabbs IIIIIIIIIIIIII
5. S. R. Marable IIIIIIIIIIII
6. C. H. Paine IIIIIIIIIIIIIIIII
7. E.M. Drewry IIIIIIIIIIIIIIIII
8. R. H. McKinney IIIIIIIIIIIIIII
9. Frank Boyd IIIIIIIIIIII
10. M. A. Gentry IIIIIIIIIIIIIIIII
11. N. S. Gentry IIIIIIIIIIIII
12. D. T. Gentry IIIIIIIIII
13. A. N. Langston IIIIIIIIIIII
14. R. M. Weaver IIIIII
15. C. T. Carter IIIIIII
16. C. B. Davis IIIIIIIIIIIII
17. D. H. Davis IIIIIIIIIIII
18. Charles Janes IIIIIIIIIII
19. R. H. Thompson IIIIIIIIIIIIIII
20. F. W. Srygley IIIIIIIIIIIIII
21. F. D. Srygley IIIIIIIIIIIIIII
22. James P. Thompson IIIIIIIIIIIII
23. John A. Thompson IIIIIIIIIIIIIII
24. Miller C. Thompson IIIIIIIIIIII
25. John A. Gresham IIIIIIIIIIII
26. Edward D. Gresham IIIIIIIII
27. G. Gresham IIIIIIIIII
28. Willie B. Parkhill IIIIII
29. Johnnie Wade IIIIIIIII
30. Eddie Ingle IIIIIIII
31. Anthony Ingle IIIIIIIIIIIIII
32. Albert Lamar IIIIIIIIIIIIII

33. J. Moore IIIIIIII
34. J. S. Kirkland
35. S. J. Kirkland
36. Willie Trimble IIIIIIIIIIIIIII
37. J. Richarsdon IIII
38. Pragle
39. Tommie Parkhill IIIII
40. G. Larimore IIIIIII
41. Theopoles Larimore IIII
42. Henry Hipel I

MEMBERSHIP OF 1879

1. K. Gresham
2. Mrs. Mary J. Thompson
3. Miss. Maggie E. Gresham
4. Elizabeth A. Gresham
5. T. B. Larimore
6. Mrs. Esther J. Larimore
7. J. C. Ott
8. Mrs. Belle G. Ott
9. L D Gresham
10. Henry Blalock
11. Mrs. Rettie Blalock
12. Miss Elizabeth Massey
13. Mrs. Mary A. Blalock
14. George W. Jones
15. Mrs. Ronnie A. Jones
16. Mallie Cox
17. Miss Frannie Blalock
18. Mary A. Gresham
19. Bettie D. Gresham

20. Mrs. Sarah Anderson
21. Amanda Wade
22. Miss Rebecca Wade
23. A. M. Parkhill
24. Mrs. Mollie L. Parkhill
25. Davidson Kirkland
26. Mrs. Alice Kirkland
27. Mrs. Mattie Morre
28. Valentine Mayers
29. Mrs. Amanda J. Mayers
30. Miles White
31. Mrs. Miles White
32. Thomas White
33. Mrs. Thomas White
34. Miss Sarah White
35. Texanna White
36. W. M. Underwood
37. Mrs. Nancy Underwood
38. James Underwood
39. W. A. Underwood
40. Mrs. Emma Jackson
41. John Underwood
42. D. P. Underwood
43. J. F. Underwood
44. Miss Amanda Underwood
45. M. M. Underwood
46. Mrs. Lue V. Underwood
47. Phillip Underwood
48. Mrs. Flora Underwood
49. W. T. Jackson
50. Lenlard Jackson
51. R. H. Thompson

52. Miss Lizzie M. Thompson
53. Mrs. Lissia E. Parks Letter
54. Edward Gresham
55. Miss Maggie L. Gresham
56. John Billingsley
57. H. Billingsly
58. W. Stevenson
59. Mrs. Harry Stevenson
60. Emily Warby
61. Miss Mallie Hamilton
62. Mrs. Martha Rackard
63. Nancy Rackard
64. Miss Almasanda Rackard
65. J. Sunnie Kirkland
66. Saul J. Kirkland
67. Harvey Rackard
68. Sydney Rackard
69. Amy Rackard
70. Sharpston
71. Billingston
72. Miss Billingston
73. Thomas Rackard
74. Mrs. Sallie Rackard
75. Harrison Worth Dismissed by letter
76. Mrs. Worth
77. F. Srygly Dismissed by letter Dec. 7, 1879
78. Mrs. F. Srygly
79. Miss Bettie Underwood
80. Mattie Kakelman
81. Jenna Brown
82. Sallie Brown
83. S. B. Snow Letter

84. Miss S. B. Snow
85. E. C. Snow
86. M. Beal Letter
87. Mrs. D. A. Beal Letter
88. R. E. McKnight Letter
89. James Pretis Letter Dismissed by letter March 30, 1879
90. Miss Fannie Long Letter Dismissed by letter April 6, 1879
91. James Cox
92. Mrs. Mary Billingsley
93. Green Cackson
94. James Broadfoot
95. Mrs. Russell Rackard
96. Columbus Wilson
97. Ledbetter
98. Mrs. Fannie Snow
99. John Walker Letter
100. Mrs. John Waler Letter

J. Gresham
   T. S. Kent Card
   Dr. Hannon

MEMBERSHIP JAN 1ST 1880 PARTIAL LIST

1. T. B. Larimore
2. Ott Clerk & Tresasurer with D. Snow
3. Mrs. P Ott
4. Mrs. Elizabeth Gresham
5. R. Thompson

6. Mrs. Jones
7. Miss Massey
8. J. Cox
9. Mrs. Cox
10. Mrs. Moore
11. Mrs. Amanda Myers
12. Mrs. Amanda Wade
13. Mrs. Rebecca Wade Dismissed by Letter Feb. 6, 1881
14. Mrs. M. Parkhill Dismissed by letter
15. Mrs. Kirkland
16. J. A. Gresham Deceased
17. Edward Gresham
18. Miles White
19. Mrs. Miles White Deceased
20. Thomas White Florence
21. Thomas J. White Florence
22. Miss Sarah White Texas
23. Miss Texana White Hudson Florence
24. H. Underwood
25. Mrs. Nancy Underwood Deceased
26. James Underwood Stony Point
27. W. Underwood
28. John T. Underwood
29. J. Underwood Dismissed by letter
30. Flora Underwood Dismissed by letter
31. Miss Amanda Underwood
32. Nelle Underwood Stony Point
33. Bellie Underwood
34. T. Jackson
35. Mrs. Emma Jackson
36. John Billingsley Dead

37. W. Billingsley joined the Methodist
38. Jim Billingsley
39. Miss Billingsley
40. Mrs. Mary Billingsley
41. W. Stevenson
42. Mrs. Nancy J. Stevenson
43. Miss Mollie Hamilston Deceased
44. Mrs. Martha Rackard Factory
45. Nancy Rackard
46. Amanda Rackard
47. Nancy Rackard Death
48. Sydney Rackard
49. S. Rackard
50. Thomas Rackard Factory
51. Mrs. Sallie Rackard Factory
52. Russell Rackard
53. Miss mattie Kackelman
54. J. B. Snow R.L. Dismissed by Teller
55. Mrs. J. B. Snow R.L. " "
56. E. Snow R.L. " "
57. Miss F. Snow Married R. E Mcknight
58. M. A. Beal R.L. Dismissed by letter Aug. 7, 1881
59. McKnight R.L. Sismissed by letter Dec. 26, 1880
60. James Broadfoot With Drawn from Ledbetter
61. Columbus Wilson R.L.
62. John Walker R.L.
63. Mrs. John Walker R.L.
64. James P. Thompkson
65. Willie Martin
66. Walter Snow Dismissed by letter
67. Clarance Frost

68. Jessed Owen R.L. Dismissed by letter Jan. 16, 1881

69. Miss Sallie M. Owen R.L. " "

70. Miss Fannie M. Snow – Mrs. R E McKnight Dismissed by letter Dec. 26, 1880

71. Charles Beard

72. Earnest Hunter

73. Miss Saleltia Swinea

74. Marion Blazton

75. W. McPeters

76. Harry Boyd

MEMBERSHIP JAN. 1, 1882

1. T. B. Larimore – pastor
2. W.H. Gresham – elder
3. Valentine Myers – deacon in Florence
4. Henry Blalock – deacon
5. Mrs. Belle Ott – dismissed by letter
6. Mrs. Esther J. Larimore
7. Miss Elizabeth Gresham
8. Miss Maggie Gresham
9. Mrs. L. D. Gresham
10. Miss Alang A. Gresham
11. Miss Bettie D. Gresham
12. Miss Maggie L. Gresham
13. Miss Minnie Thompson – Dead
14. R. H. Thompson
15. Mrs. Ronnie A. Jones – Died in 1890
16. Mrs. Sarak A. Anderson
17. Mrs. Bettie Blalock
18. Miss Elizabeth Massey

19. Mrs. Mary A. Blalock
20. Miss Fannie Blalock Willis
21. Janet Cox
22. Mrs. Mattie Cox
23. Mrs. Mattie Moore
24. Mrs. Amanda Myers – in Florence
25. Mrs. Amanda Wade – Deceased
26. A. M. Parkhill – Dead
27. Mrs. Parkhill – at Savanna
28. David Kirkland – Dead
29. Mrs. N. Kirkland
30. S. Kirkland
31. Sammie Kirkland
32. Edward Gresham
33. Miles White
34. Mrs. Miles White
35. Tango White – in Florence
36. Miss Sarak White – Dismissed by letter
37. Mrs. Texanna Hudson – In Florence
38. James Underwood – Stony Point
39. D. P. Underwood – Stony Point
40. J. F. Underwood – withdrawn from
41. W. Stevenson – at woodland
42. Mrs. Nancy J. Stevenson – at woodland
43. Miss Mollie Hamilton – Departed this life
44. John Walker – Deceased
45. Harry Boyd – in Tennessee
46. F. J. Denson – at Stony Point
47. Mrs. Ellen Denson – at Stony Point
48. Marion Ernest – moved to Texas
49. Mary A. White – in Florence
50. Nancy U. Rackard

51. T. A. Gresham – Dead
52. Saletha Swinea –
53. M. Underwood
54. Mrs. Nancy Underwood-Departed this life May 1883
55. Phillip Underwood
56. Miss M M Harris – Stony Point
57. Miss Bettie Harris
58. Miss Green Jackson
59. Mrs. Emma Jackson
60. Tarva Underwood – Departed this life Aug, 1882
61. Miss Busby Cluade – Moved to Lawrence County
62. Mure Uyres – Florence
63. Charlee Pope
64. Eugene Phillips – Moved off
65. Charles Sharp – Dead
66. Willie Parkhill – at Savanna
67. C. Sharp – Florence
68. Mrs. Polly Sharp – Dead
69. W W Vick – Letter
70. F Vick – Letter
71. Mrs Martha Fenn
72. David Sharp – Florence
73. David Sharp
74. Janey Balckburn
75. Charles Sharp
76. Miss Mary Taremore
77. William Stevenson
78. Miss Annie Blackburn
79. Owen Sharp – dead
80. Miss Martha Craven

81. Tany P Thornton – at Bonun Tesea, Dead
82. Mrs S. Underwood
83. Miss Racael Sharp
84. Miss M Blacburn
85. Thomas House
86. William Sharp – Florence
87. Mrs. Baugh
88. T. Underwood – at woodland
89. Robert Claybourne – Florence
90. James Haddock – Dead
91. James Sharp – Florence
92. James Fenn – Marked off
93. Laura Fenn – at woodland
94. Whitten – in Tenneesee
95. Florence Thompson – Ne Henry died March 23, 1891
96. Lillie Sharp – in Florence
97. Lane Moore
98. Eddie Blalock – Hord, AL
99. Maggie Blalock
100. M. Bosie – in Florence
101. Robert Mayers – in Florence
102. Robert Mayers – in Florence
103. Lee Sharp – in Sheffield
104. Esther Gresham
105. Carrole Sharp – in Florence
106. Miss V. Moore
107. H. Larimore
108. Theo Larimore
109. Granvile Larimore
110. L C Moore
111. Ile C Thompson – Deceased

112. John Blackburn
113. W. Blackburn
114. C. Ringlesteen – at Stony Point
115. Catie Ott
116. Ettie Larimore
117. Emma Gresham
118. Fannie Cravin, Fizzie Craven
119. Albert Moore, Ana Moore Tooie, Peda Blalock

MEETING OF AUGUST 5, 1894

Henry Blalock, Jr.
- J. George
- Genvie Blalock
- I Holland
- Mrs. R. H. Thompson
- M. McCafferty
- Mr. McCafferty
- Eddie Fenn
- Willie Jones
- Omie Jones
- Eddie Underwood
- Mrs. Underwood
- Miss Moore
- Mrs. Claud Moore
- Velma Moore
- Mattie Racherman
- Avery Thompson
- Miss I Thompson
- Miss Bell Blalock
- Miss Esther Blalock
- Rufhus Blalock

Perry Anderson
Miss Eminola Morrison
Miss Helen Morrison
W. Rickard
Mrs. S. L. Pinck
L.D. Rikard
J. H. Rikard
A. P. Rikard
Rome Rikard
Lula Moore
Gwen Thompson
Hattie Biglow
W.M. Bamlett

List of Ministers

T.B. Larimore — 1871–1857
Jesse Ehrman Thornberry
Everett Oscar Coffman
James C. Keaster II
Paul Simon — 1949–1955 (FindAGrave)
Kenneth Byron Davis — 1959—1960 confirmed (*Florence Times*)
Robert Waller — 1960–1963 (*Florence Times*)
Kenneth Odell Davis — 1965–1982 confirmed, (*Preachers of Today, Churches of Today*)
Larry Gooch
Randy Baker
Tim Grigsby
Jack Wilhelm — 1998–2006 (obituary)
John Paul Heupel — 2001/2002–2004 (*Times Daily*)
Bill Bagents — June 2000 – March 23, 2020
Cory Collins — 2007–?
Mark Marks

Chris Moran — 2012–2023 (Facebook)
Matt Burgess
Rickey Collum — 2005–2007, 2023-present

Photographs

MARS HILL SCHOOL, SPRING OF 1914—Mrs. Mabel Lancaster, 1915 Chisholm Rd., Florence, spent more than three more years of time to identify a photograph made on a spring day long ago. Top row: Louie Moore (Posner), deceased; Ester Blalock (Harrison); Irene Thompson (married name unknown); Ruth Blalock (married name unknown); Emmett Clark. Middle row: Adalia Mae Anderson (Jaxton), deceased; Ollie E. Heupel (Smith) deceased; Rosie Koehleman (married name unknown); Whitney Blalock, deceased; Moore Phillips, deceased; Thompson boy; Jacob W. Heupel, killed in World War I; Miss Annie Poole (Hitchcock), teacher, deceased. Bottom row: Esther Anderson, deceased; Giselle Kaphleman (married name unknown); Ova Phillips (Thornton); Mabel Heupel (Lancaster); and Earl Anderson, deceased.

[From the collection of E. T. "Buck" Jaynes, presented to Mars Hill Church of Christ, 4/2/2002].

New Mars Hill Meetinghouse
(1904 - 1976)

AN EARLY HISTORY OF THE MARS HILL CHURCH OF CHRIS...

AN EARLY HISTORY OF THE MARS HILL CHURCH OF CHRIS...

AN EARLY HISTORY OF THE MARS HILL CHURCH OF CHRIS...

C. WAYNE KILPATRICK

AN EARLY HISTORY OF THE MARS HILL CHURCH OF CHRIS...

Paintings of the Old Building by Various Artists

C. WAYNE KILPATRICK

www.ingramcontent.com/pod-product-compliance
Lightning Source LLC
LaVergne TN
LVHW040153080526
838202LV00042B/3143